To Martha
Good Fr
Joyce & Clarence

MW01051893

OUT OF
THE AIR
AND
ONTO
THE GROUND

The Clarence Davids Story

Clarence Davids Jr.

Jer: 29:11

OUT OF THE AIR

AND

ONTO

THE GROUND

The Clarence Davids Story

CLARENCE DAVIDS SR.

Packaged by WinePress Publishing, PO Box 428, Enumclaw, WA 98022. The views expressed or implied in this work do not necessarily reflect those of WinePress Publishing. Ultimate design, content, and editorial accuracy of this work are the responsibilities of the author.

ISBN 1-57921-188-7
Library of Congress Catalog Card Number: 99-63451

Contents

Prologue

I love working with the earth and elements to help God create His awesome splendors. Had I never persisted in joining the Army Air Corps during World War II, the opportunities to be one of the Master's skilled workers in the field of landscape design and management never may have happened. As I reflect back, it is clear to see how the Lord nudged me along and opened the doors of destiny. My course was set when an Army officer reassigned me from flying as a gunner on a bomber, to ground duty in the US Army/Air Engineer Corps. He took me out of the air and put me firmly onto the ground—a decision that would determine my life's work.

For this, I give all the credit to God.

CLARENCE DAVIDS SR.

Chapter One

To the Land of Opportunity

I f it had not been for a wooden shoe hitting the side of a
teacher's head, I may never have been an American.
Turn-of-the-century Holland was a harsh place for a
headstrong boy with ideas of his own. Klaus Davids, my
dad, was expelled from school in the fourth grade for using
his shoe as a means to exert these ideas. I'm not sure what
issue transpired between him and his teacher, but I do know
my dad always had a knack for making situations work to
his advantage. Hitting the teacher with his shoe only con-
firms to me that Dad was born with a flair for independent
thinking. This character trait, although defiant and disre-
spectful as a youngster in the Netherlands, later worked in
his favor to survive as an immigrant in America.

He never told me why he hit the teacher. I suspect he
was not proud of what he had done, and his son didn't need
to know the shady details. Perhaps he thought that it would
only confuse and clutter my thinking. After all, there was

just too much work to be done in the new homeland to dwell on negative moments of the past.

Dutch families are notoriously close. Close almost to a fault. Many things that happen within family circles never go outside the house, and so I never pressed my father to tell me any more of his past than he had to. I had tremendous respect for him.

My dad's family was low Dutch, from the province of Gronigen. Like most folks of this area in Holland, the Davids (*Davouds* in Dutch) were poor people who could barely provide for themselves. Soon after being forced out of school because of his behavior, Dad's parents put him to work as a farm hand for the Boers (wealthy Dutch farmers). At ten years old, he became a migrant worker much like the Hispanics and Asians in America. He slept in straw cots tied to the walls of the workers' shacks, and he worked from daylight until dusk, six days a week. The only reprieve he had was the freedom to choose the farmers he would work for, and he left many jobs because they were meanspirited and brutal to their work hands.

The Boers ran their operations with meticulous but steel fists. Workers, especially ten-year-old malcontents, were driven with one goal in mind: production. Dad learned the hard way what a day's work meant.

Klaus Davids spent nearly ten of his formative years in this near slave-labor environment. In all these years of working, he never had meat to eat. The farmers would eat the meat and dole out the speck (fat) to the workers to live on. By the time he was nineteen, Dad had saved enough money to leave the miserable life in the Netherlands.

He grew through his teenage years, working and helping the family survive the very lean economic times that the Netherlands experienced at the turn of the century. During these years of hard and sometimes abusive labor,

Dad could think of nothing else than having an opportunity to put in a day's work that he could call his own. He had never worked for himself; all his work had been only for someone else. By instinct Klaus knew that if the people he worked for could rise to where they were, and have what they had, then he could do it too. He also had just the right character and determination to use the right circumstances and hard work to make the change.

The Davids have always been churchgoing people. Dad was a Christian from an early age and regularly attended Sunday services with his family. However, his commitment to the faith began to wane some when he went off to work the Boer farms. I know he spent what little free time he had, skating on the canals in the winter.

During his late teens, Dad met a young lady by the name of Minna Bonda. It was springtime and the ice had melted on the canals. Skating the canals was on hold for another season. Church was a good alternative for something to do on my dad's days off, and it was at a church social that he met the lady who would become my mother.

As they courted and drew closer together, my dad shared with Minna his dream of going to America—the land of opportunity. She was immediately excited and fell in step with him to share his adventurous thoughts of leaving for the land of opportunity.

Dad's brother had come to America a couple of years previous, and he was a source of encouragement. He had been able to purchase his own farm and paved the way for my dad to make the trip.

The courting couple made a plan. Dad would come to America and settle and work until he had enough money to make the trip back to the Netherlands to marry Minna and escort her back. With everything settled, he departed by ship.

Arriving in New York, Dad made his way to the Chicago area where his brother Carl lived. He soon had a job working at the Western Electric factories where workers assembled telephone switchboards and other components. Western Electric eventually became AT&T. He worked as an assembly line worker because he spoke hardly any English, and this was the best he could find. His pay was minimal, to say the least.

My dad was always a man who needed a mountain to climb—something to challenge him. Even as a lowly line worker, he dared to be different. At Western Electric there was a rule that no one could put on his hat before quitting time. If you did, it was a sign that you were done for the day. To add a flare of controversy, and perhaps a bit of defiance, Dad always put on his hat ten minutes before the quitting-time whistle blew. They would reprimand and even threaten to fire him, but he stuck to his guns and made it a personal crusade to put on that slouchy old hat and work for the last few minutes of every day. I'm sure that he had it a little cocked to the side just to punctuate his special quest.

It was a difficult year for a young man in love. With Minna thousands of miles away and separated from him by the Atlantic Ocean, he dreamed of marrying her and raising a family. His misery would have been worse had he not thrown himself into his work. He had an incredible way of networking with people, and during that time, he not only was making money, he also was making important connections that would lead to his lasting success in Chicago.

He worked a year at this job and finally had enough savings to go back and retrieve his bride.

The return voyage to Holland was uneventful, but his homecoming was special. Minna was even more beautiful than before, and she had arranged for the wedding to happen as soon as he arrived. She wanted out of Holland as much as any other poor Dutchman.

He was twenty and she was nineteen, and the small Reformed Church congregation made their wedding day one of the happiest days of their lives. Even though Minnie's parents were happy to see their daughter wed, it was still a sad occasion for them because they knew their youngest daughter was leaving for foreign lands with her new prince.

Their honeymoon was spent on the voyage to America. Mother was not in the best frame of mind to be a bride, though; she stayed seasick for the entire trip. When they arrived in New York, she actually got down on her hands and knees and kissed the ground. She said, "I'll never go back again."

They were married for more than fifty years, and I had the wonderful privilege of being the MC at their fiftieth wedding anniversary.

Turf Builders—Steps to Success:

- Never allow your lack of education to stop you.
- Make the most of every opportunity.
- Be willing to do work others will not do.

Chapter Two

Cashing in on Garbage

When World War I broke out, it was to my dad's advantage.

Not long after returning to America with my mother, he left his job at Western Electric and went to work for a man named Bill Venema. Bill had owned a garbage-collection route since coming to America from the Netherlands, and it was profitable.

At the turn of the century, the lousiest job anyone could have in Chicago was being a garbage collector. It was a job given only to the immigrants, and Venema cashed in on the opportunity. When he approached my dad, there was no hesitation; he jumped at the chance to work for this man of success. With Dad's zeal it was not long before he had learned the ropes, and the business became a natural for him.

Venema had become a wealthy man in the garbage field, and he was very good in the business. Because he had money when he came over from Holland, he was able to secure his own horse and a wagon, and it wasn't long before he began getting garbage accounts for weekly pickups. He had one route, and it had made him a fairly wealthy Dutchman.

However, his patriotism got the best of him. When the war broke out in Europe, Holland became militarily involved. Being Dutch and feeling like it was his duty, Bill Venema decided to return to the Netherlands and join the army to fight.

Venema was Dad's best buddy, and he was a single man at the time. He had no one to leave his business with, so he and Dad struck up a deal. Venema said, "Nick [my father had changed his name to Nick Davids by then], if I don't come back, it's yours."

In the process of putting his affairs in order, he handed over the proprietorship of his garbage route to my father. Venema told Dad, "All I want when I come back, the Lord willing and my life is spared there, is my garbage route back—exactly what I gave you. But, if you have established any other routes and have bought wagons on your own, they are yours, Nick. This is my payoff to you for keeping my business going for me in my absence."

It was the only cue my dad needed to go into action. This was the moment he had waited for and the opportunity he had come to America in search of. He could finally own his own business!

Well, Bill Venema didn't get killed, and he did return to take his route back, but it did give Dad enough time to get his own business established and operational. With Venema's garbage route already fully functioning and profitable, Dad was able to save his money to buy a second horse with a wagon and start another route.

During this time my mother, Minna, had become the master of our household, and over the next several years

16

had a child about every other year until there were seven of us. With seven children at her feet and my dad working nights and sleeping during the day, she became our stable influence. I thank God that she was a strong Christian and imparted much of these values in us at an early age. But this also had its downfall.

Mother was better educated than my dad. She never hesitated to read us Bible stories and other stimulating and healthy books. I owe much of my sensitivity toward Christ to her and her diligence to make and keep a godly family atmosphere at our home. However, the God that I knew as a child is different than the one I know today. The God that mother portrayed to me was a fearful, punishing Master. His heavy hand of punishment for rowdy young men like me seemed always to be over my head. I did not like this aspect of learning about the Creator of the universe. Because of this, it took me a long time to really accept the Lord as my personal Savior. In our church services, the minister preached only hell, fire, and damnation. It was an unhealthy fear of God, and it took me a long time to get over it.

My dad on the other hand, left spiritual teachings to my mother. He was, however, a self-educated man and very wise through practical experience. I know Dad loved God, but he was an extremely focused businessman, and I was taught much about life by just watching him work and network with others.

By this time, my dad had succeeded in the garbage business. He had made the transition from horse and wagon, over to trucks, and this streamlined his business considerably. He had a growing garbage business, and this gave him more credibility in the city. His influence among other businessmen was considerable.

One particular highlight of knowing my dad as a businessman was the time when he organized a charitable event with several other Dutch immigrant businessmen.

He helped them form an association to assist the less fortunate people in the community. It was put together strictly out of the sense of compassion and a desire to share their wealth with others.

This group of giving and people-loving men would put on a special picnic once every summer and gather all the needy people in the neighborhood and have fun and food. Together with those who were well off financially and those who had hardly anything but a roof over their heads, we would turn an ordinary Saturday into a celebration that I know Jesus loved. My father's association of hard-working Dutchmen provided everything free of charge. It was wonderful.

One character trait that was ingrained in me through my father was the fact that if you are successful, you should never hoard or be miserly with what God has given you. I learned at an early age to share my blessings with others.

Turf Builders—Steps to Success:

- Be willing to advance yourself when the opportunities arise.
- Fear God for the right reasons: remember He is love and died for you!
- Success relies on how willing you are to give—not on your desires to receive.

Chapter Three

In My Father's Image

1923 was an interesting time to be born in Chicago, Illinois. The Great Depression had not hit yet, but my early years were spent in an economic depression of considerable magnitude for most people. Because my father created his garbage business with such dedication, we were not stricken with poverty like most families.

Chicago was deluged with immigrants at the time of my birth and early years. We lived in the Dutch community on the west side of the city. This area was meshed together with nearby Italian, Jewish, Polish, and African-American communities, and it seemed as though we all had our own little countries—a melting pot of the world. Different languages were spoken; the celebrations had their own ethnic flavor. We loved our own types of food and carried on many of the old-country traditions. But most importantly, each nationality had its own work to do, and many of the disagreements—and sometimes outright wars—were sparked when one ethnic community invaded another's area of occupation, or means to earn a living and survive in this new country.

Much is said these days about the degree of hate among different ethnic groups in our large cities. Hate crimes are on the rise now more than ever. However, when I was a boy, we did not hate the people of other national origins. We simply did not associate with each other because of the vast differences in our language and living styles. Oh sure, when I was a young man, I would go looking for excitement with my Dutch companions. For fun (or sport) we would go into the other neighborhoods to test ourselves against the Italians or Jews. This was usually after having a few drinks. And if we really wanted a challenging fight, we would go across Ashland Avenue into the Black community. However, our motives were not of a prejudiced spirit, but merely from the challenges and intrigue of living in such a diversified patchwork of cultures.

It was during my childhood that I witnessed the melding together of all these nationalities into the greater Chicago area. I saw the Dutch families (my family being one) move from the West Side to Cicero, to Berwyn, the North Side, the South Side—all over the city. I saw the Italians merge into the other areas of the city as well.

I remember a radio host by the name of Howard Miller who would broadcast the same message everyday. He would preach integration even before it was popular. He would say, "If we could only break up these ethnic communities and mingle ourselves together . . . this ain't Dutch, this ain't Polish, this ain't Italian, etc., etc. . . . Man how we could live in peace with each other!" Partly because of advocates like Mr. Miller, Chicago today is a unique blend of many people living in peace.

During this time my dad continued to expand his business in the city of Chicago. Consequently, my family found itself living in many neighborhoods over the years. We went where Dad knew best to settle because of business strategies. He worked methodically, and this attributed much to the successful businessman that he became.

In the late forties, not long after I was discharged from the service, my dad finally decided to retire. Selling the garbage business, which he had built it into a nice business, he could have retired comfortably. However, like I am today, it was not in him to sit still for long. The world still had too many challenges left.

Just shortly after retiring from the disposal business, he became enamored with another business that he enjoyed. Right after the war (WWII), candy was a scarce commodity in America, and Dad took the right steps to fill needs, as he always was so good at doing. He bought a candy delivery route and began working it. He loved it because it proved to bring joy to others.

At this time he was in his late fifties and evidently was not ready to be put out to pasture. When he heard of the candy route being up for sale, he knew it was for him. He bought the route and the Pollyanna Candy Company had just acquired one of the best networking salesmen—Nick Davids—and didn't even know it.

Dad loved this candy route more than any other business he had ever been involved in—not because it made money, but because it made people happy. This is where I learned to love my dad's heart more than ever before. It was here I learned that if you can make people happy with the work you do, then you cannot fail in anything that you set yourself to do.

He would go to the wholesale warehouses, pick up assorted candy, and retail it to schools and other institutions on a route that was established. He particularly liked the Catholic schools. He once told me, "I've never had so many sisters in my life!"

Having this candy route was the epitome of the American dream for Nick Davids. It was not a franchised business, but a business that depended solely upon the owner's creativity and will to succeed. He bought it from an independent fellow who had established the candy delivery route to all the Catholic schools on the north side of Chicago, and Father turned it into more than it had ever been before.

I remember Father's basement being jam-packed full of candy of all kinds. He even had stocks of cigars for him and his friends to smoke. They, too, were purchased at wholesale prices, and he loved to share what he himself enjoyed; a good Dutch Master's cigar.

It is very clear to me that I have inherited my dad's savvy for business. Not only do I enjoy the work of making a business run like a clock, I like making friends and doing good for the people I serve.

Turf Builders—Steps to Success:

- If you can make people happy with your work, then you cannot fail in anything you set yourself to do.
- Never retire—just work with a change of scenery from time to time.
- You are never alone in business if you include your family.

Chapter Four

A Good Foundation

I have learned that with any building and construction project, foundations are the most important. The same goes with the "foundation building" of raising a family. The spiritual foundation that my life has been built upon is a very valued thing for me. It has been a blessing to have a good spiritual beginning to lean on now that I am older.

There were nine people in my family: six boys, one girl, and my parents. Both of my parents were leaders in their own ways: my dad in his work and my mother in caring for the family as she did. Both were devout Christians and good church people. Dad served several years on the Christian school board. We rarely missed going to church on Sunday, and Sunday school was mandatory for us.

Even though I can thank God that I had such a good beginning, church was not always an enjoyable experience for me: partly because I had so much energy that it was hard to behave the way I was expected to behave and also because, the church we attended was extremely rigid.

The first minister I remember, during my days of going to church on the West Side of Chicago, was a stern man, and I always saw him as being very unfriendly. I suppose the punishment I was getting from my parents in the pews didn't help my attitude much either.

It was important to my mother that we all sit very still during the services. She didn't put up with any nonsense, and since I was always fidgety and a little hyper, I had the honor of sitting next to her most of the time. It was nice at times to snuggle up to her fur collar, but this near proximity also had its liabilities; I received some awful pinches when I got out of line.

Growing up, we also had a lot of rules in our home. For an example, playing games, such as Rook, or even baseball, was not allowed on Sunday. Another rule concerned how we dressed. We were dressed up for church and had to keep these clothes on for the entire day. As you can imagine, this restricted us from doing many activities that we wanted to do. These rules were made to obey, and if we did not obey, we paid. The consequences were the usual corporal punishment that ruins your whole day.

Our church had three long and boring services. The early morning service was in English, and the one in the afternoon was in Dutch, and then again in the evening there was a service in English. The only time any of us kids had to go to the Dutch service was when we were naughty. With all my talking out of line and fighting with my brothers, I spent a lot of time in the Dutch services.

I always tried to make a good experience out of the bad ones, and eventually I found a certain affinity for the Dutch services. I liked to sing, and in this particular service they sang more from the heart, and the louder the better seemed to be the byword.

One unusual thing I remember about these songs is that they all had peculiar endings. Instead of ending on a lower note, they ended on high notes. I enjoyed singing these songs. Since I was a very active kid and received much discipline, I had a lot of opportunities to sing in Dutch, and got quite good at it.

As I got older, more rules came about. One was the practice of observing the holy day, or the day of rest. There were a lot of rules connected to what we could or could not do on Sunday. This influence was very strong in my life, and I remember once thinking that one of our garbagemen was a hypocrite for going to work after leaving church on Sunday. It wasn't until many years later that I finally found freedom from these rules about Sunday.

It seems like many of the rules were meant to keep us tied up and to toe the mark. I have never quite figured out the reason for some of them, even to this day. In light of this, I still have to believe that they were originally established for the good of people . . . by good people. Perhaps they went askew over the years serving to control and manipulate people.

I attended a Christian school from an early age, and here again my views of Christianity became slanted in a negative way. We were inundated with Bible and religion. It seems as though the teachers highlighted and dwelt on the dos and don'ts, more than they did on the love, peace, mercy, and grace of God. I can clearly remember thinking that when I got older I would make decisions on my own without any influence from heavy-handed authority. Then, as an adult, I would not include all these rules and regulations in my Christian life. I suppose, even at that early age, I knew in my heart that I would live in the truth someday, and if it took unshackling myself from some principles formed by man, then that's what I would do.

I have never been good at memory lessons. Before each catechism mother would make sure that I knew the lesson. She expected me to have it memorized by heart, but having a memory problem, I never did catch on to this form of learning. In fact this led me to an incident in church that typified my life at that time.

I wore a Dutch cap to these classes, and it was just big enough for me to carry a small book inside to peek into. I knew it was not right to do such a thing, but it was fun and made learning (or passing) a lot easier. When it came to education, I looked for easy ways to do things.

One Friday evening class, I was called on to answer. When I did answer I must have given my "hat trick" away, because the thing he asked was, "What do you have in your cap, Clarence?"

"Eh, my cap? Why?" I stammered.

When he began to walk toward me, I knew I was caught, so I quickly admitted, "I have a book in my cap. . . ."

"Have you been reading that book?" He queried me again.

"Could be," I replied.

I did not want to say yes, because at that time the catechism teachers had a right to hit us, and I was afraid he would. Besides, he was an elder in the church and took his duties of teaching very seriously.

Then he advanced the rest of the way to my desk and opened my cap.

"You were reading!"

"I s'pose I was." I answered.

He looked down at me and said, "You didn't admit it!"

I sort of smiled and replied, "Well . . . kind of."

"Clarence," he said, "that is not admitting it. If you do something wrong, you should admit it."

I ended up being sent out of the class and then home to Mother. This was my greatest fear. Dad left all the discipline up to her, and she made each of us—from the youngest to oldest—"toe the mark." Mother made it very clear to all of us that she could tie all of us up into little knots and throw us to the wild animals if she wanted to. As a mother she would never allow us to suffer harm, but she could sure scare us enough to gain our respect when we got into trouble.

I was often the topic of discussion between my dad and mother. My unruliness frustrated them many times. Often they came to me, with Mother doing most of the talking, and attempted to rectify my behavior. I became good at giving them empty promises, and they did extend grace to me many times. However, I look back now and can see that I got out of these problems with my folks by using parent-pleasing phrases.

It was as though the rules were keeping me from finding the freedom I knew was part of being a Christian. With this in mind my rebellion and naughtiness continued. As I look back, I do regret any trouble I caused when I was younger, and I only mention this period of my life to show the power of God to make changes in a person's life.

As an illustration of my rebellious nature and unruliness, I will share an example: One evening while attending a young men's class at church, I along with some other boys, was running through the basement making a lot of noise. The church janitor caught us and tried to get us to slow down and be quiet, but we ignored him. When he left we headed for the kitchen and there we found all the preparations for the church meal. We proceeded to take all the salt shakers and put sugar in them. We then took black pepper and mixed it in with everything.

After we were satisfied that we had accomplished our mission of mischief, we realized that we were almost late for our class, so off we went running again. As we neared the classroom, I was running so fast that I could not slow down enough to stop before colliding into the glass door. I was going so fast that I ran right through it, shattering glass all over the classroom floor. The teacher and other students were spellbound with disbelief when it happened.

I looked at the teacher and said, "I opened the door, and the glass broke." It was obvious what I had done, but because I was so defiant, I felt that I could get them to believe anything.

After the teacher regained his composure, all he could say was, "You went right through it, Clarence!"

With my smart attitude, I turned and looked at the door, and asked, "Did I?"

The teacher then did the appropriate thing to get my attention; he sent me home to speak to my parents. This was not an easy thing to do, and after a grueling lecture session—the kind only my parents could conduct—I did a lot of dishes and missed many allowances after that night.

Reflecting on my adversity to rules, regulations, and the stiffness of church activities when I was a child, I must say that I was probably leaning toward trying a different slant on religion at a pretty early age. In fact, most of what I remember church and social life to be as a child was a pain in the neck. It was difficult for me to see the love of God back then. I am now blessed beyond belief that as an adult Christian I have found the freedom I believed was always possible. I have found that Christianity is not rules and regulations; it is a *relationship* with Christ. Since gaining this freedom from religious stiffness, my life has been motivated through mercy, grace, and charity.

Turf Builders—Steps to Success:

- Rules are *not* made to be broken; they are made to be improved upon.
- Honor and obey your parents. If you do, all will go well with you your whole life.

Chapter Five

First Steps

I was born the second to the last out of seven children, and as a kid, I loved working with my dad in his business. I worked on Saturdays to give my brother Carl a break because he worked fulltime for Dad. I always thought I spent too much time as a youngster taking care of my younger brother, Jake, but it was part of my chores and expected of me. I did not resent Jake for it, but did have my priorities of interest, and working a business was at the top. At any rate, when I did get the chance to work with Dad in his business, I enjoyed it a lot. The work was hard, but even at that early age, I could see that the disposal business that Dad was so proud of was something special for our family.

One trait peculiar to the Davids family is a work ethic and a persistence to overcome challenges. This did not make working for my dad an easy chore, but I did learn a lot. I remember once I was trying to lift a barrel up onto the truck and I told him, "I can't do it!" He literally kicked me off the truck and said, "Figure it out! No Davids ever says 'I can't.'" I stopped and thought a moment, and with him looking on, I went around to the other side of the truck and grabbed a shovel. I then proceeded to empty half of the can out onto the dock so I could lift it onto the truck. I then shoveled the remaining half back into the empty can and dumped it as I had done with the first half. Dad patted me on the back and commented, "That's a Davids for you . . . using your head."

From that point on, I have often figured out a way to do what seems to be impossible. It may have been a difficult lesson to learn at the time, but it has proven to be invaluable in my own years of business, studies, and work.

When a tragedy strikes families, many dynamics get shaken up. Dutch families generally have a unique way of dealing with family problems and accidents. They just close the doors and keep to themselves. The first tragedy to strike the Davids family was a sorrowful one.

I was five years old when my brother Ted was killed in an accident. He was nine years old and full of life when he slammed into a taxicab on a sled. This death made the winter seem even more dreary and ominous for our family. For me, Ted's death served as a benchmark, and it caused me to form some unhealthy views of life and death. These views and attitudes stuck with me until I was well into adulthood.

In those days it was more economical and customary to keep the body of deceased relatives in the home. The caskets were placed in a particular room of the house until the burial. The funerals were right in the home, but until the time came for the official burial and ceremony, the family members took turns sitting with the body. I was too young to sit with Ted's body, but I did have a bedroom right next to the room with the casket in it. I had to pass the casket every time I wanted to go in or out of my room. This scared me so bad that I never went to any funerals after that for over twenty years.

At the age of twelve I came down with a serious illness and my stomach became infected. Surgery left a large hole in my abdomen, and I remained sick for quite a while. I lost much weight, going from 140 pounds down to 65. I was as good as dead.

The doctor told my parents there was no hope. The next thing I knew, my dad was making plans for me to come home. The doctor informed him that I would surely die at home, and my dad replied, "He'll die at home, not in a hospital."

"How will you get him home?" the doctor asked.

My dad answered, "In an ambulance."

"He will die if you do."

My dad looked at the doctor and quietly said, "That may be, but he will not die in the hospital."

I was in a coma at the time and woke up about a week later and found myself in my sister's bed, surrounded by family and relatives. I asked my mother, "Ma, what's going on? Why are all these people here?" She then told me that they had come to be with me in my passing.

From that moment on, I began healing. However, I did have a hole in my stomach that wasn't supposed to be there. I cried out to my parents. I remember pleading with them to send me to Doctor Rottschaeffer; he was a doctor who I knew could help me. "I want to go to Dr. Schaeffer," I would cry. "Maybe he can put a stitch in this hole. I don't want to be like this all my life." Something in my spirit was telling me that Dr. Rottschaeffer was God's man to use to heal me.

My parents listened and took me to this doctor. When we arrived, I was almost surprised at Dr. Rottschaeffer's confidence that he could make me better. I believe even to this day that the Lord Jesus was orchestrating this meeting, because a miracle was about to happen. Dr. Rottschaeffer merely said, "Lay down, Klaus, and pull down those pants." The next thing he did was take a simple septic pencil—the kind used for razor nicks—and began to apply it all around this hole. It burned like the dickens, but it worked. The hole shrunk to hardly anything in a matter of just days. I now have a big scar to remind me of God's goodness in healing.

When I experienced this miraculous working of God in healing my body, my life began to change spiritually. The change was subtle and gradual, and the influence of being raised in a Christian home slowly began to have more impact on my life.

I didn't feel worthy of being saved like that by God. I was not a criminal as a young man, but I did do things that I was not proud of. While some of the kids my age were stripping cars and stealing, I was into fighting. I took up boxing to vent my energy into something that I could not get in trouble for; however, I still did not feel as though I was deserving of such grace and mercy by God.

I think it was the second time that God performed a healing miracle for me that I was finally convinced that He liked me. I knew that He was interested in saving me for His service later on. Now as I look back, I can see why He took the time to spare my life. He had more plans for me.

Almost a year after the stomach problem, I was riding my bicycle on the boulevard with a friend. It was a two-lane street, and my friend and I entered the street and were riding very close to one another when our bicycles collided slightly, and the next thing I knew, I was being thrown into the air. I had been run over by a car.

The car that hit me was a funeral vehicle. It was the kind used to carry flowers to gravesites. As I wove slightly out into the lane, the fender hit me and threw me out in front of the car, and I hit the pavement. As the car was about to run me over, I moved my body just in time to prevent having my head being smashed like my brother Ted's had been when he died. Both tires of the car ran over my left leg and crushed it instead. The car then drove on; I was a victim of a hit-and-run accident! Fortunately I was able to see the license plates and remembered the number to identify the automobile for the police.

Another car stopped, and the two guys in it saw me sprawled on the pavement in front of them. I thank God for people who are like the Good Samaritan. They stopped their car and blocked traffic and began redirecting other cars around me. These two young fellows also called the police and ambulance. The fellow driving the funeral car was soon caught and booked for hit and run.

Just as the ambulance arrived to tend to me, I called to my friend, "Elmer, get my folks! Get my folks! Tell them that they are taking me to the hospital!"

I know that God was directing the minds and hands of the ambulance drivers, too. They had enough sense to put a stick splint on my leg before moving me. They had no idea how bad it was because it was wintertime, and I had pretty thick pants on, but they were not taking any chances. It was a good thing they did, or I probably would not have a left leg today.

At the hospital (the same one I was in before) I was laid out on the operating table. By now my family had arrived, and they were there to support and pray for me. They arrived just in time to hear a nurse say, "Don't pull the boot off; his leg is only being held by a thread of tissue! Cut the boot instead!" Here again, I believe that God was using a person as His spokesman to care for my well being and to orchestrate the healing I needed. If the doctor had pulled my boot off instead of cutting it, he would have pulled my leg off; and back then it was not likely that any medical techniques could have saved a leg.

The leg was sewn back and then set again, but they did not put a cast on it. I'm not sure what the medical thinking was about this, but it didn't work too well.

I have always been a rabble-rouser, always looking for some excitement, and one highlight of my stay in the hospital was when I invited all the kids from my class at Timothy Christian School to visit me. They were supposed to come in only four at a time, but I figured out a way for them all to come up to my room via the fire escape. With forty kids or so in my little hospital room, we had a grand time—until we got caught, of course. I never have had a hard time being popular and having exciting fun. To many of the Dutch kids, I was a leader in my own right. I think I set the record in that hospital for the most visitors for any one patient.

Seven days after the accident, I was released from the hospital, and the doctors were all amazed at how rapidly my leg had healed up. One doctor commented to my father, "He has so much calcium in his body that he heals faster than most. He can go."

I was home only a few days, sitting in the kitchen with my mother, when she saw the minister coming up the walk.

She jumped up and said, "Quick, go to the living room. We can't have the minister in the kitchen. Hurry!"

As I was hurrying over her very slippery, polished floor, my crutch snagged on a rug and I fell and rebroke my leg. I was rushed back to the hospital where I was kept for another two months.

To set the leg properly, they had to drill a silver spike into the bone above my knee. I was then put in traction with weights and pulleys to help keep the leg immoveable and able to heal properly. When it was time to remove the spike, the doctor did not have the strength to pull it from my leg. One of my brothers—Mike, who was visiting me—had to pull the spike out.

Now I was ready to go home, and they finally put a cast on the leg. One memorable thing about this time is that my nurse was the girlfriend of George Goble, the-country-and western star. George happened to visit right before I left the hospital, and he and the nurse both signed my cast. After they did this, the word seemed to get around in the hospital and all the nurses on three floors of the hospital came one by one and signed my cast. I felt pretty special about this.

Since my mother never learned to drive an automobile, she had to take a bus to visit me, and she never missed a day. She was a committed mother, and I am thankful to God for her.

Mother continued to try to discipline me as time went on, but there were times when it did not work, and matters only got worse. For an example, I remember one Halloween when I was about fourteen years old. My buddies and I decided to sneak our sisters' long, wool socks out to use for clubs to hit people with. We filled them with flour, and when someone was hit with them, it would not hurt them much, but it would shower them with white flour.

That evening we were standing in a group at a corner, preparing to slug passersby with our flour-filled bludgeons. One of the guys who was getting there late did not know that an Irish cop was there questioning us about our socks full of flour. They were out of sight from our newly arriving buddy, and he did not know the cop was with us just around the corner. He decided to come around the corner swinging at us, and he hit the cop instead. The cop, with white flower covering his dark blue uniform, began swearing and swinging his billyclub.

We all bolted in every direction to keep from being hit, and in the scramble, I fell to the ground and landed on my left arm, breaking it at the wrist.

After getting away I made it home and told mother that my arm had been broken. She acted as though she did not believe me. She was so angry with my rebellion that she grabbed my arm and slammed it down on the table, and it broke again in the upper area. I know she felt bad about it, but she never apologized or let me know that she had made a mistake in her off-handed disciplinary action. My father was horrified at this incident and took me immediately to the hospital.

As I grew into my middle teenage years, I became more and more serious about my work. At the age of fifteen I gladly quit school and went to work. School actually was very difficult for me, possibly due to ADHD (Attention Deficit Hyperactivity Disorder). Memorizing was extremely difficult, and most of our teaching required large amounts of memorization. Little did I know at that time that later in life, I would be back for more schooling and education—with a lot more appreciation for the whole process! However, my conclusion at the time was that school was holding me back from making a success of my life.

Soon after I quit, I got a job delivering telegrams for Western Union. I got plenty of exercise delivering messages all over the downtown Chicago by foot and bicycle, but I knew it was a dead end for me. It did lead to other jobs. One day, as I was delivering a telegram to the *Daily News* paper, the editor liked the way I conducted myself (I always was neat and courteous in my work) and said, "You looking for a job?"

"I have a job . . . this one." I replied

He smiled and said, "No. I mean are you looking for a better job? I like the way you conduct yourself. Pick up an application and fill it out."

I did get the job and worked in the newsroom, gathering all the ticket tapes that came in from all the horse-race results around the country. I would then make sure that they got organized for printing in the daily paper. It was a good job.

Later I went to work at the factories of Western Electric making eighteen dollars a week. This work lasted until I went into the Army Air Corps in WW II. Western Electric was the same company that my father had worked for when he first came over from the Netherlands, but he had nothing to do with my getting hired. It was during the Depression, and the only way one could get hired was to be recommended by someone who worked there. I had a friend whose uncle worked on the assembly line there, and he was responsible for getting me hired.

My friend was a year younger than I, and we were two tough guys, and we both loved to fight. Neither of us knew who could whip the other. One day we decided to find out and fought until we could fight no more. It finally ended in a draw. We shook hands and became the very best of buddies. He then enlisted into the Marine Corps when WWII broke out. It impacted me a lot to see him leave; he was as close as any brother could be.

Turf Builders—Steps to Success:

- Serve others first and put their priorities before your own, and you will profit much.
- Believe in miracles, and there will be many.
- Put your life and work into the hands of God, and He will sustain you.

Chapter Six

A Dutchman in Love

It was this same close buddy who was with me when I met my future wife. We had just come out of a tavern on the south side of town, and he'd had more drinks than I and was getting pretty loud. I figured it was time to leave, so started to drive off. It was then that I noticed a couple of girls by the curb, so I pulled over and stopped.

Not recognizing one of the girls, I began talking to the one I had seen before. Her name was Jeanette. After a few words with her, I decided that she would be a better match for my friend, so I backed off and let him take over the conversation. Turning my attention to the strange girl, I introduced myself, and my life began to change on the spot.

It was a good thing I was dressed neatly that day. It looked as though I had been to church, so the girl was receptive and introduced herself back. "My name is Josephine Klemp."

My friend and Jeanette decided they wanted to go somewhere on their own, and I was somewhat relieved. Now I could get to know a little more about this Josephine girl without any distractions. I offered to buy her a hamburger, but she was not interested. Instead, we sat in the back of the car and talked for almost an hour about who we were and about our lives. It was good, and I really liked her.

I met her again about a week later, but this time I had been drinking a little more than she liked, and she was not as open. I invited her to take a ride with me in the car, but she refused. So I got out and we talked again as I walked her home.

At her house, she told me that she was not going to ask me in because I had been drinking. This came as a challenge to me, and I set about to see if I could scare her into letting me come inside.

I told her, "If you don't let me in, I'll throw a brick through your front window."

"Are you kidding me?" Her eyes revealed that she did not know whether to believe me or not.

"Yes, I'm kidding." I admitted.

"Do you want to see me again?" she asked.

I told her that I did very much, and she went on to inform me that if I ever wanted to see her again that I would have to go to church to find her. She would only meet me there and nowhere else. God sure has unusual ways of getting his children to get right with Him. I realized that I had fallen in love, and going to church was a small price to pay for the approval of Jo.

Turf Builders—Steps to Success:

- Be slow to judge others, especially by what they look like and what they do for a living.
- Be willing to yield your own desires and idiosyncrasies in favor of someone else's ideas and suggestions.

Chapter Seven

The Davids in the Depression

The 1930s, or the Depression Years, as they are called, was a period of time in which people struggled with many difficult situations. As I look back at the Great Depression, I have mixed emotions.

It was almost an unheard-of experience for many of the WWII generation to actually have more than they needed. Our family was unusually fortunate in this respect. The Davids had more than most, but we also had a large capacity to share what we had with those who were not so fortunate.

In 1930, I was in the second grade, and we lived in a poor neighborhood. To illustrate what our life was like there, I recall a time when I was invited to my friend's house for lunch. Even though I knew the boy was poor, I did not refuse the invitation because I did not want to hurt his feelings. When I returned home, my mother asked me where I had been and when I told her I had eaten at the boy's home, she scolded me for eating what precious food these people had to offer. I then described my meal while I was their guest. I told mother that I had a half glass of milk along with a piece of bread with some real good tasting white stuff spread on it. She then explained that this was salted lard. At the time I did not mind if it was lard; it tasted good, and that is all that counted.

Our family was financially secure, but we were also rich in love for others. We had an ample supply of God's imparted love to share with those around us. Every evening during these depressed years, our family would gather around our dinner table. It was not just a time to eat, but it was a time also to discuss the condition of the various families we knew in our church. We would talk about what they needed, and together we would figure out what we could do to help them.

Frequently our neighborhood/community would have clothing drives, with everyone pitching in to provide something. Dad had a flair for helping people. The Davids enjoyed going through the closets and storage to find clothes. We would then pile the Buick full and take them to a family in need. To see tears of gratefulness was always reward enough for everyone in our family as we drove away.

I saw much love during these years and truly believe that it set a special place in my heart for helping others. Our generation was not a complaining generation, and it was one that learned to love through adversity. We grew strong because of the enormous struggles in everyday life, but most of all, we learned to work and take care of each other.

We did not have the luxuries of today's society and were blessed in our own way for that. World War II may have had very different problems, and perhaps we would have had different outcomes had my generation not gone through the Depression Years. We were all uniquely ready for the war years that followed. As young men and women who had to work very physical jobs, we were conditioned for the rigors of war and supporting it. Women who went to work in the factories and assembly lines were already used to working for long hours each day. My future wife, Jo, and I both had assembly-line jobs just before the war broke out, and we knew what a good day's work meant.

Through the sadness and loss of the Depression Years, I have seen how God has redeemed those awful years into something good. I look back and see many fun things our family did. If there had not been for bad times, we may never have had those opportunities.

The Lord truly does work in adversities.

Turf Builders—Steps to Success:

- Give thanks to God in everything, and hold tightly to those values that are good.
- When you are having a bad day, find someone who is worse off and help them. If you do, your day will be better.
- When life is tough, consider it training for the future. God does have a plan for your life, and He has ways to prepare you for the process.

Chapter Eight

Out of the Air &
Onto the Ground

The years that followed the Great Depression were years of training for me. I had many delightful experiences and some not delightful. One was the automobile accident that nearly left me a cripple. One good thing about having a leg nearly ripped off as a kid is the possibility that I was no longer a candidate for military duty.

My childhood injury did not happen to be an asset for me, however, because I *wanted* to be in uniform serving my country. It did not take me long to realize that my old injuries and health problems were going to present additional hurdles that I had to jump over in life—especially when it came to enlisting in the armed forces.

World War II had arrived, and my desire to enter military service was at an all-time high. I had one brother-in-law serving in the army, and Carl, my older brother, was in the army cavalry at Ft. Riley, Kansas. I visited him while he was in training in Kansas, and I was surprised to see that the army was still riding horses. And to top that off, Carl and the other troops wore swords and were training with stick rifles instead of real guns. The United States was terribly unprepared for this war. Carl was later transferred to the Quartermaster Corps. My younger brother and I were also convinced and determined not to stay out of the fight. We both longed to be in uniform.

When the war began, Jo (who had become my steady girlfriend by then) and I were working steady jobs. I was at Western Electric, and she worked at Pullman Electric. She had won my heart, and I had become a regular church attendee. We always hear the saying, "God sure must have a sense of humor." Well, I can vouch for that saying, and it sure is true in my case. God knew my inner desire was to be married to a Dutch gal and raise a family, so He put Jo in my life to draw me closer to Him. I never missed a Sunday service after she told me that the only way I was going to get to know her, or even see her, was in church. She laid down the law, and her strong resolve in the matter only convinced me more that she was the one meant for me.

The assembly line at Western Electric was good, steady work for many of the Dutch people during and after the Depression. We valued our jobs, and none of us liked the thought of seeking relief from the government. To a Dutchman, a soup line was nearly unthinkable. It would have shattered our pride to resort to a handout when there was work around.

My closest buddy, with whom I used to box with, did not waste any time enlisting in the Marine Corps when the Japanese bombed Pearl Harbor. As always, he was up for a good fight. He was inducted and went off for his service to the West Coast. He was always an adventure seeker. When he left, I also tried to go in; however, two different doctors refused to give me a physical report that any of the service branches would accept.

Both doctors I saw told me that I would never have the stamina for marching and training. With my previous injuries and infirmities, they not only feared that I would never be able to stand up to the rigors of military life, but also were concerned that I would have presented dangers for those buddies who would depend on my physical strength to pull them through from time to time. I understood their points of view, but I knew my limitations, and in my mind, I was as healthy and strong as any one else.

I was determined to go. My mother kept telling me that I was classified 4-F and that I should forget about the military and stay home. I was not hearing any of that, nor was I going to be a "second-rate citizen" by being 4-F. I was convinced her reason for my remaining a civilian was because she already had a son and son-in-law away for military duty. If she could keep me home, all the better. She was very protective of us.

My determination grew with every passing day. Like a bulldog, I kept showing up at the induction center, hoping that I could convince someone there that I was fit for duty. Finally one of the doctors that had given me a physical examination on my previous visit got tired of seeing me there. He called me aside and said, "I'm going to send you to have a talk with the colonel; he's the doctor in charge here." He signed a piece of paper, and handed it to me. "And you watch your *ps* and *qs* while you are with the colonel. He has the final say-so in matters like this."

The colonel's office was separate from the other areas of the induction center. It could have intimidated most people. I suppose I should have felt special about getting an exam from the chief officer of the center, but I was so determined to enter the military that nothing was more important than passing the exam to get inducted.

The colonel was a very direct man. As soon as I entered his office, he pointed at me and said, "OK, strip off your clothes and let's have a look."

He began examining my leg and pushed in several different places. He then looked up at me and said, "It's your decision. You can either serve or go home. I'll honor whatever choice you make. However, I would suggest that you stay home; you will be able to serve better as a civilian."

As I began putting my clothes back on, I announced my decision to him. "I'm not going to stay home. There's a fight going on, and I have never backed down from one yet."

He closed my folder and handed it to me: "OK. You're in. Good luck."

As I followed him into the adjoining room, he spoke over his shoulder to me, "Which branch do you want to serve in?"

"Marines." I replied.

"Marines! Man, you will never be able to stand up to the marching, running, and all the physical demands they put on you. The army either. The infantry is no place for a guy with a leg like that. They just won't accept you."

I was thinking of my boxing buddy when I replied, "You've gotta be kidding! My best buddy is a marine, and I want to serve with him."

"I'm sorry, but I think you should try something like the navy, Davids."

My eyes widened as I spoke, "No sir, not me. I'd rather have dry ground beneath me when the shooting starts."

"Well, if there is an opening, I can perhaps get you into the Army Air Corps."

I cut him off. "I'll take it! I've always wanted to fly, anyway."

I was walking on cloud nine when I walked in the house. My mother could tell that I had gotten my way, and immediately she began to cry. I didn't tell her that they rejected me, and that the only way I made it was by getting my foot in the colonel's door. If she had known, I'm not sure that she may have gone to have a talk with the colonel himself. If she had, I'm afraid my chances of going may not have been so good. Back then, a mother sometimes had more power in the decisions of what happened to her kids! My mother was very protective—and convincing!

I went to Western Electric and gave them notice that I would be leaving their employment for military service. I have always been one to make sure that my affairs are in order, and as an employer now, I know how important it is for employees to keep me appraised of any changes that may effect their working status.

To my surprise, I was not only given their permission, but the management decided to subsidize my military pay. They offered to pay me the difference between my military salary and what I would have been making had I stayed and worked on the assembly line. They were figuring in all the raises that I would receive in that time period too. I accepted their offer and thanked God for His provisions as I closed out my matters there. I received this subsidy for nearly three years, and at the end of my military service, I had around three thousand dollars saved at home in the bank. This was a lot of money to have in savings at the time, and it helped me get a good jump on what I had to do with my business when I got out of the military.

I was sent via troop train to Miami, Florida, for my basic training. The reason Miami was chosen as a training area was because we were practicing for invasions from the water. Many of our exercises focused on water landings and other amphibious maneuvers. The part I liked most was serving as a lifeguard for the others. My job was to be on lookout for sharks and men-of-war, which presented a constant danger for us.

Then I was shipped to Sioux Falls, South Dakota, for schooling. Going from Florida and then to South Dakota by train was the first time I had done any traveling on my own. I was excited for the new adventures I was experiencing, but on the other hand, I felt an emptiness I had never felt before. I knew I would miss my family, but most of all, I was missing my girlfriend, Jo.

At the army training base in Sioux Falls, military living was austere and Spartan, to say the least. As World War II broke out, these bases swelled in numbers of personnel, and the accommodations had not been upgraded to handle so many troops in one place at one time. Wood barracks were crowded with bunk beds—so much so that it was difficult to walk between them. The food was OK, but nothing like my mother's cooking back in Chicago. With the strict hours, training schedule, and GI food, many soldiers began to lose weight and physically trim down. I always stayed in good shape with my hobby of boxing, so I maintained well.

Throughout the training period, all of us were constantly wondering about what kind of jobs we would get once we got out of basic army training. Occasionally, personnel clerks and personnel officers would pull us from the ranks and go over certain possibilities. I'm not quite sure what aptitudes or physical indicators they were looking for in each of us, but they seemed to have a method.

I was called into personnel and informed that I was slated to be a radio operator/waist gunner on a B-17 bomber. The type of gunner I was to train for was the man who operated the guns in the bubble on the top of the aircraft. The corps was in need of them.

I was then told that my duty station would be in England, and I would be flying missions over Europe from there. I was disheartened to find out that the great need for these gunners was because they lost so many on every mission that was sent out.

I began radio school after basic training. In this school, I learned some very valuable things. I learned Morse code and became proficient at it. The way they trained us to keep our radios operational was to take them and smash them as though they been in a plane crash, and we were expected to put them back together so we could send a message for help. If the plane went down, the radio operator was the key man because he was responsible for getting the word back to base that they were in need of rescue.

It was dead winter when I went through my training in South Dakota, and it was extremely cold and miserable: sub-zero weather. At the very end of the radio school, I became ill with pneumonia. It is always a tough thing to say that God gives us an infirmity, but as I look back He definitely did not want me to go to England to fly in B-17s. He had another plan for my life.

I became only slightly ill at first and went to sick call. The army doctor diagnosed it as a "slight" case of walking pneumonia and merely gave me some aspirin and sent me back to duty. I was sitting in class, feeling worse as the day went by, and by the time three days had passed, I had a full-blown case of lobar pneumonia. I remember lying on my bunk and not being able even to get up to go to the bathroom. I really felt as though I was going to die right then and there. I had never been so sick.

An army ambulance had to come and fetch me. This time when I got to the hospital, it was full of soldiers who had come down sick; there was an epidemic. However, since

I was in worse condition than most, they found a bed for me and began medicating me with sulphur pills.

As the hours passed I got worse, and they took me to an isolation ward. This was the place where the hopeless cases were taken. Here I was virtually left to die while the doctors tried their best to save the healthiest of the sick in the other wards. I went into a coma, and all was given up for me to survive.

The army sent a letter to my mother, informing her that I was seriously ill and that she was urgently advised to visit me. She later told me that she worried that I would die before she could get to me. Mother notified Jo, and together they set out by train for the Sioux Falls Army Training Base.

Once again God intervened and saved my life. By the time mother and Josephine arrived, not only had I come out of the coma, but also I was released from the critical/isolation ward. When they saw me sitting and playing cards with some of the other soldiers in the hospital, Jo's first comment to mother was "I knew that sucker would be playing cards."

With tears of joy, they hugged and kissed me, and I realized then how much they both meant to me. We had a wonderful visit.

In the midst of all the greetings, visiting, and closeness I goofed. Like most men, I discovered one of my blind spots when it comes to the opposite sex. I kissed Josephine a few times and failed to let her know that I loved her. I suppose I was taking it for granted that she would know that I loved her if I kissed her, but when it comes to women, nothing should ever be taken for granted.

She never mentioned how this affected her during her visit, but when I got a tear-stained letter explaining how it made her feel, I felt like a heel. Since that time, I have done my best to be courteous and thoughtful to all women, especially the one I'm in love with.

After mother and Jo left, I was released from the hospital to find out that my class had already been shipped to England, and I was once again standing in the personnel division building.

"Well, what are we going to do with you now, PFC Davids?" the tall personnel officer spoke from the other side of his desk. "With your lung condition and other physical problems you do not need to be in a combat-related unit."

He was right. I was out of gas. My strength had waned during my stint in the hospital, and I knew that I was going to have to look in another direction besides flying in airplanes.

He looked over my file and then looked up and said, "Private, I'm going to change your classification again; I'm going to get you out of the air and onto the ground. How would you like to be an engineer?"

This sounded pretty good . . . and important. With minimal confidence I asked, "But, sir, what if I don't have the schooling to be an engineer?"

"The army will handle that," he replied.

Turf Builders—Steps to Success:

- If you persist in your communication, you will do well in life. "Ask and you will receive . . . knock and He will answer." Try, try, and try again.
- Let go, and let God. If given full access to work, God will take care of your every need.
- Never take other human beings for granted. God has given each person a point of view and the capability to succeed within their limits.

Chapter Nine

Far Eastern Duty

I have always enjoyed outside work. The new duty and reclassification proved to be just incredibly important to the rest of my life.

The army transferred me to another training post into Georgia to be trained as a heavy-equipment operator. Being an engineer was not what I thought it meant. Always before when someone mentioned an engineer, I thought of highly educated people who are like scientists. I figured they were the smart ones who worked out and planned the details for the operational management of large projects, or the design and manufacturing of products. When I arrived and began training to be an Army Air Corps engineer, I was relieved to find out that it meant that I would be building roads, landing strips, bridges, and buildings. I would train to run bulldozers and other pieces of construction equipment. I was definitely given "ground" duty.

The school was a great learning experience for me. I soon found an immense enjoyment out of creating and molding the earth with the big machinery. We trained primarily for putting in landing strips and airfields for the bombers to operate from. Since these larger, heavily loaded airplanes always needed more runway than fighters, we drilled and drilled on how to move a lot of dirt and grade large expanses of area.

At the end of our training, we were loaded on trains and shipped to the West Coast. Arriving in San Diego, we boarded a navy transport ship and set sail for the Far East. My unit was the 25th Air Service Group and our final destination was India.

This was a terribly long trip—sixty-five days. I found out the hard way that the ship had not been cleaned while it was in port. My very first night, I was bitten from head to foot by fleas, and after that I decided that a bed was not for me. I slept on the deck in a hammock the rest of the way.

Days turned into weeks aboard the ship, and like anywhere else in the military, when there is not much to do but wait, boredom becomes your worst enemy. Our activities were limited to playing cards, cleaning up the ship, and . . . boxing matches.

When I heard that the command was scheduling boxing matches and looking for boxers, I jumped at the chance. I had loved boxing all my life, and ever since the days of street fighting in Chicago, it had become one of my prime interests in athletics. I worked hard at being the best boxer I could be. I volunteered to be one of the fighters and spent a lot of time working out. In all the fights I had on board the ship, I lost only a few during the entire voyage.

We finally reached Melbourne, Australia, and it was so good to go ashore. The Australian people were very cordial toward the American servicemen during World War II. They were so grateful that we would travel so far and use so much of our machinery and manpower to keep the Japanese from invading and conquering their country. Many Australian families had sons fighting in Europe, Africa, and other parts of Asia, and when we showed up, they took us in like long-lost sons. It was wonderful.

From there, we sailed on to Perth, which is on the West Coast of Australia. This would be our last stop before setting out across the Indian Ocean to Bombay, India.

The Indian Ocean, at that time, was one of the most treacherous stretches of water in the world—not because of storms and other natural encumbrances, but because it was crawling with Japanese submarines armed with torpedoes. Allied freighters, tankers, troopships, and other naval tactical vessels were "sitting ducks" and prime targets. Everyone always dreaded crossing it.

I'm not sure, to this day, if we were just lucky or if God had put the Japanese U-boat crews to sleep while we were at sea. We never had one shot fired at us—not even a false alarm.

We pulled into Bombay, which is on the West Coast of India, and disembarked there. Our destination in India was Calcutta, and to the uninformed, it would appear that we had gone the long way around. However, it all made good sense. The Bay of Bengal, the waters of Calcutta harbors, were infested with Japanese ships and submarines. To go into those waters was like walking into a deathtrap, so the Allied Commanders ordered all traffic to Calcutta to arrive at Bombay and then move by train to Calcutta.

The train trip was long and very hot. We were like packed sardines, and there was no such thing as air conditioning on Indian trains. Most of the soldiers stripped down to t-shirts and shorts and traveled the entire distance that way. At night we constantly fought the mosquitoes along with the suffocating heat.

When we arrived just outside of Calcutta, all of our machinery was waiting. We blazed new roads through the jungle in order to get to the area where we were to build the new airstrip for the bombers that would be making the runs "over the hump." (*Over the hump* was the term used for the airplane route across the mountainous areas of southern China to Japan.)

We worked long, hard days getting this airstrip ready for the bombers to use. I acclimated fairly quickly, and before long was able to work the entire day in just shorts and boots. However, many of the men had to be more careful with heat stroke and sunburn.

Malaria was my biggest concern. I didn't want to contract this deadly disease because it was a lingering, sometimes lifelong malady that I did not wish to put up with and endure the rest of my life. We lived in large squad tents and had mosquito netting around our bunks, but no matter how well we defended ourselves against the hungry little critters, we always got bit. Many of the men got malaria, but I never did; perhaps God had His hand upon me once again, and I thank Him to this day.

After months in India, we finished our job and received orders to return to Bombay again. We loaded up our personal gear and boarded the train again for the long journey across central India. By this time we were ready for a change of pace. We had survived the heat, the mosquitoes, the baboons, wild dogs, and other prowling animals that constantly were trying to get to our food supplies.

Once in Bombay, we set sail across the Indian Ocean again for Perth, Australia. Our destination this time was a small island in the Pacific called Tinian. This island gained its fame for being the launch base for the B-29 bombers that carried the atomic bombs to Nagasaki and Hiroshima, Japan.

Tinian Island is on the fifteenth parallel just north of Guam in the Mariana Island group. It was approximately six hundred miles southeast of Japan. Because of its strategic location, it had been chosen as the base that would launch the aircraft carrying the two bombs that forced the Japanese to surrender. This resulted in a rapid end to the war in the Pacific.

While on Tinian, an unusual surprise happened. My mother kept a pretty good stream of correspondence coming to her three sons who were serving at the same time. I did my best to keep her posted in spite of the censorship we had on our outgoing mail. In one of her letters she mentioned that the names of the streets where we were stationed were the same that Carl was mentioning in his letters to her. I asked around and found out that there was a quartermaster outfit on the island, and did I get excited! *Could Carl be stationed on Tinian too?*

I borrowed a Jeep and got some time off and set off to see what I could find out. I soon found the quartermaster unit, and after identifying myself as Carl's brother, they directed me to his tent. I found him sleeping and was he surprised to see his younger brother. We had not seen each other in over two years, and we had a wonderful reunion.

A bit of irony is that we found out later that Jake, our younger brother, who was stationed on a navy destroyer had been part of the crew that was responsible for the shelling of Tinian before we got there. He and his shipmates had helped secure the island for American occupation. It was a good feeling to realize that we were all on the same team and working so close together so far away from home.

I worked on the end of the runway. I was there when the flights carrying the atomic bombs took off. I didn't know what the plan was, other than it was very secretive, very dangerous, and heavily guarded. It is sort of strange to think that I saw the planes take off, but I never saw the results until after the war was over. I saw the devastation in a movie theater in downtown Chicago after I became a civilian again. I wept with everyone there to see what this mission had done.

I am proud to have served in such a critical capacity. Many people today believe that the use of the atomic bomb was inhumane and atrocious. They fail to realize that had America not dropped those bombs, the war with Japan could have lingered for years, costing many, many more lives than we can imagine. The Japanese military was committed to fighting to the last person, and surrender was an unthinkable thought. We may have had to kill many more people than we did had we not sent them a powerful message in superior war technology.

On Tinian our unit improved runways and helped clear runways when bombers would not make the takeoff due to overload. At the same time, we were always enlarging the runways for the larger aircraft. It was around-the-clock work and dangerous, but we got our work done and were proud to serve in the way we did.

Finally, the curtain fell on the Japanese military machine. The two bombs were dropped and the leaders of Japan knew they could never stand up to such technology and force. They wisely chose to surrender.

I have no regrets about the work I did to help my country preserve our rights and freedom. I am also forever grateful for the experience I received as a member of the US Army Air Corps.

Turf Builders—Steps to Success:

- If one is patient and can wait for God instead of getting out ahead of the Creator, he will have his dreams fulfilled
- You will always find a use for past skills and hobbies. Do not take them lightly.
- If you can see all sides to an issue before forming an opinion, your success is imminent.

Chapter Ten

Welcome Home

At the end of the war, we were still on Tinian Island and ready to go home. The only problem was that there were no ships available to transport us back. This caused many problems for the servicemen stuck in places like Tinian. We lodged so many complaints and refused to do work for so long that President Truman finally issued specific orders to get our boys home. We had faithfully served our time, and now it was time for our country to serve us by getting us home as soon as possible. Truman gained my admiration by the steps he took to expedite the means for our return.

The ship I returned on did not go to the West Coast like many of them did. We came across the Pacific and went through the Panama Canal. From there we sailed north to New York. The trip was uneventful, and we all welcomed the peace and rest.

New York City was a lively place at the end of the war. Everyone was joyful and had new dreams of getting things back to normal. When we disembarked from the ship, the town came alive. Even though it was still a big, dirty city crammed with people, It seemed like a paradise to us GIs who had been away for so long.

A group of us decided to see the town and began walking the streets, looking for some excitement. We hopped from bar to bar and dive to dive for several hours. It was a great time. In one of the bars, a man approached us and told us that he was a representative from the Phil Pastami All-Girl Orchestra. He had orders from Phil himself to search the city of New York for GIs that had just returned from the war and sign them up to sing for his show.

I had played guitar and my sister played the mandolin when we were younger, so there had been a degree of musical talent in our family. We agreed to sing for the show and it was a real fun time for us.

It was Christmas time when we arrived in New York, so Phil had all of us singing, "I'll be home for Christmas," and I thought it was ironical because we were already home, and here we were on national radio wishing we were. It was all we could do not to laugh. I enjoyed this as much as my love for boxing.

I'll never forget Evelyn, the magic violin player with the orchestra. She was wonderful to get to know, and I'll probably never see another person play the violin so well. I still have her autographed picture. Singing with this group and being recognized nationally was a special highlight in our welcome home.

After a couple of weeks, I left New York and caught a train back to Chicago. It was good to be home for Christmas, thanks to President Truman for making it possible. His ordering every available ship to serve as troop transports, showed me that he was a man who cared about the servicemen and women and that he kept his promises.

I reported into Camp Grant, Illinois, and spent a few days mustering out of the service. I was honorably discharged from the armed forces February 26, 1946, and had attained the rank of corporal. I suppose I would have easily been promoted to sergeant had I reenlisted, but attaining a new wife and the adventures of a new enterprise awaited me as a civilian.

When I got home, I was itching to strike out on my own. I was ready to use some of my military experiences as an equipment operator to get into my own business. However, my mother had other ideas.

After the welcome home and rejoicing, she told me that I had no choice but to go back to the Western Electric assembly lines. She reminded me that they had been good enough to subsidize my pay all the time I was away; the least I could do was go back and honor them with my continued employment. I didn't want to go back, but she was right; I did owe them my services.

This was a frustrating time for me. I had been working outside with the land for so long that I didn't think I could ever adjust to being back inside. I had been excavating, grading, and bulldozing in the army, and now I felt a call to continue working like that. I wanted to obey my mother and do right by Western Electric, so I laid down my own desires to honor her wishes. This is what God would have all of us do, because He will make things happen without our help. I just had to be patient and do what was right.

One thing that was very unsettling was the lack of welcome home from our church. The first soldiers returning from WWII were cheered much more. By the time I came home in 1946, too little was said.

My fiancé, Jo, had been waiting for my return and wanted to get married. However, she was cautious. She had heard rumors that some GIs were returning home not right in their minds. Some had also picked up venereal disease or malaria.

She told me that she wanted to wait three months to see how things went with me before getting married. I agreed! I thanked God that I had a job to return to during this time period. Her parents were also watching to see if I was going to go to work or just be a lazy man who thought the world owed him a living.

After being home for three months, Jo kept her word and we were wed.

The following year was a challenging time for me because we had to live with her folks. Once again, we were grateful for their willingness to help us get started, but we felt our desire to start our own family in a strong way.

Now that I look back on it, I was very blessed to get the military training. It had given me an edge on civilian work ethics. The discipline and training in the Army Air Corps had given me a new standard to practice in the arena of work. I appreciated this in my civilian work because it helped me provide better for my family and future.

Turf Builders—Steps to Success:

- *Sequence of work priorities:*
  1. Always work according to what God calls you to do.
  2. If paid, do that work next.
  3. If your work has been promised, do that work next.
  4. Then, lastly, do the work *you want* to do.
- Always pay your debts—regardless of how large or small.
- Honor your mother and father, even as an adult, and all will go well with you.

Chapter Eleven

Getting Started

The year was 1951, and I worked nearly that entire year on the assembly line, but my mind was elsewhere. I knew that Western Electric was no place for me. I knew that after working outside with the earth and elements for the past three years, an inside job was not going to work for me. Even the thought of doing the same job inside a factory over and over each day and year would probably drive me over the edge, and I knew that I would be in trouble. I prayed to God for perseverance daily.

Don't get me wrong; I was very grateful for all that Western Electric had done, but I had a burning desire to get started with my new life. It was upon my mother's desire to see that I did right by those who had helped me that I faithfully went each day to a job that my heart was not into. I did my best to honor her concerns. My father, on the other hand, understood and sympathized with me. He, too, had worked at Western Electric before starting his own business, and I had his support and encouragement from time to time on stepping out and getting started on my own.

I finally bought myself a used car and did not have to rely on catching rides to work with others. Jo and I felt as though we were making headway. However, when she announced that she was pregnant with our first child, this added another pressure for me to be stable in my work. I could not help but voice my frustrations to her about how dissatisfied I was with factory work, but she was always concerned about us having a stable income. I understood her concern, but this still did not put out the drive I had to step out and do something on my own.

Always thinking about improving ourselves, Jo and I decided it was time to move away from her folks. With the baby coming we needed to have a home of our own. We rented a gift shop with an apartment, and Jo ran the shop. This did not bring in much money, so we took our savings (four thousand dollars) and paid cash for a mobile home in a mobile park. We could have bought a brand-new home in a development for nine thousand dollars, but we chose not to go into debt.

In my spare time, I watched the papers. I was looking for anything that seemed like an opening or opportunity for me to check. One day I saw an ad in which a man was requesting the services of a landscaper.

I didn't know much about what a landscaper does, but I did know that it was outside work. My heart leapt, and I could feel an excitement inside that told me that this was something that I should investigate. I followed my hunch.

Since my father knew a landscaper when we lived in Cicero, I called him and asked, "What is a landscaper?"

He had a good laugh, and said, "Why, he's the guy who cuts lawns, trims bushes, plants shrubs, and all that. He also puts in grass seed and makes lawns grow for people."

"Why, I could do that!" I replied.

My father was always an encourager for me, especially when it came to figuring out how to get ahead in life. We spoke more on the phone, and after I hung up I was more convinced than ever that I could do the work of a landscaper.

I responded to the ad and called the man, whose name was George.

"George? Clarence Davids here. I'm looking for a job."

He was a pleasant man and easy to talk to.

He then asked, "Have you ever done this kind of work before?"

"No sir," I said. "I have not, but I can tell you one thing, I can outwork any two men that you put beside me. I just got out of the war, and I need to put some of my experiences of the Engineer Corps to practice."

"Oh," he said. "You're a vet?"

I said, "Yes sir, I am."

I wasn't sure if he was for veterans or against them. Some folks back then were like Jo before she married me. Many were very cautious about trusting responsibilities to war veterans. But I was confident, and I believe he detected this over the phone and liked it.

"Are you a church man?" he asked.

"Yes sir. I've been raised in a Christian home all my life."

"Davids . . . is that a Dutch name?" he inquired.

"No sir," I said. "It is a Scandinavian name, but I'm a Dutchman. My folks were both born in the old country and came from the Netherlands around the turn of the century."

"Well," he said, "why don't you come on over and see me. Perhaps you will do."

When I went over to see him, I noticed that his house was right next door to a Christian Reformed Church. I was encouraged to see this. He invited me in and immediately announced that he was going to hire me.

"On the basis that I'm a vet?" I asked.

"No," he said, "on the basis that you said you could outwork two men, and on the fact that you are a Christian. I've lived next door to this church for years now, and I think they are wonderful people. I'm a Catholic, but I've never seen better or harder-working people in all my life. And I know that you are honest. You've got the job."

This was the basic foundational decision that started Evergreen Landscape Company.

Turf Builders—Steps to Success:

- Never overstep the capacity to pay your bills. Debt is no way to conduct business.
- Never cease looking for ways to improve yourself, your family, and your business.
- Remember, your reputation precedes you in everything you do. Your name is more important than your wealth, possessions, and desires. "A good name is to be more desired than great riches." (Prov. 22:1*a*)

Chapter Twelve

Back to the Earth

George was a good landscaper and hard worker. I enjoyed learning the art of landscaping from him. He was quite a bit older, and I considered him to be my mentor in this exciting new work.

I was happy to be away from the factory work at Western Electric and doing outside work. I had almost forgotten what it was like to breathe fresh air all day long and to work the ground and watch God make my work grow. I spent my days cutting, trimming, digging, raking, planting, and even doing some landscape design that George supervised. He was happy with my work and commented on how fast I picked up the knack for landscaping. I was a happy man.

George was a key person in my rise to success in the landscape business. I owe a lot to him in getting me started in the business.

All the basics that I know today came from him. He taught me how to bid jobs and how to get the correct terminology for plants, equipment, and techniques. Working with him expanded my interest in many ways. I took it upon myself to take courses at Purdue University in Indiana on Saturdays. I acquired some knowledge in the field of landscape and gardening. I could not get enough of it, and my focus was intense.

After two months of working at George's side, I was feeling very confident that this was my place in life. One day as we were taking a lunch break, I asked him, "George, are you looking for a partner?" I knew by instinct that one never gets anything unless one asks for it, so I boldly stepped out and popped the question to him.

"Ya know," he smiled, "I've been thinking about that. I think we could do pretty well together, Clarence."

I asked again, "Well, what do you think? Is there a possibility that we could become partners?"

"I think so," he replied, "but it's going to cost you."

I had never bought into a business before, so I was not sure what to say from that point, so he kept right on.

He thought about it a second, scratched his chin, and said, "I think I could cut you in for, let's say, seven hundred dollars. What d'ya think? We could be equal partners if you can raise the money."

It was a partnership that I could not, or would not, refuse. It was a joining that would change my life and bring me to where I am today.

I had enough money in savings to cover the price he wanted, so I consulted with Jo, and we agreed that this was money well spent. It would hopefully set in place a means for us to advance in life and increase our earning power. But most of all, I think she knew that this was going to succeed because it was something that I had a passion for. She knew, as well as I did, that without passion for your work, you may as well not do it at all.

Turf Builders—Steps to Success:

- Be willing to take risks. Faith is not faith without an element of risk.
- Express what is on your mind to those around you, and you will find that those expressions will take on new life.
- Find a mentor—someone who will teach you, love you, and hold you accountable to your commitments.
- Work with passion, or don't work at all. Acceptance of mediocrity is a license for failure.

My parents Nick and Minnie Davis with me and
my siblings. Left to right –
John, Mike, Ann, Carl, Clarence and Jake.

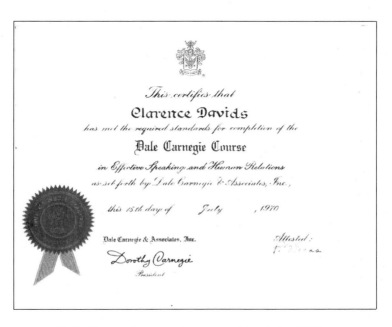

Dale Carnegie award received in July 1970.

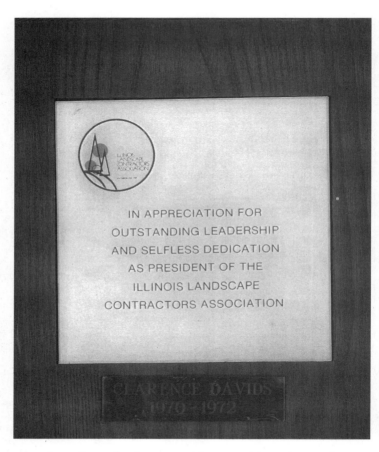

IN APPRECIATION FOR
OUTSTANDING LEADERSHIP
AND SELFLESS DEDICATION
AS PRESIDENT OF THE
ILLINOIS LANDSCAPE
CONTRACTORS ASSOCIATION

CLARENCE DAVIDS
1970-1972

Award received as outgoing President in 1993.

Concerned Citizens Party

OF EVERGREEN PARK, ILLINOIS

PRESIDENT

CLARENCE DAVIDS, SR.

CLARENCE DAVIDS, SR., 49, Candidate for Village President, resides at 2836 98th St. with his wife Josephine.

Clare and Jo have been residents for the past 21 years and have four children and two grandchildren, Clarence J., Jr., Barbara De Boer, William J., and Sandra Jean. Clarence Jr., his wife Paula, and their two children also live in the village. Barbara's husband PFC Jay De Boer is in the service. The David's are members of the Evergreen Park Christian Reformed Church.

Mr. Davids is a graduate of Timothy Christian School, attended various college courses in business administration, and served 3½ years in the U.S. Air Corps. He is the Chairman of the Board of Clarence Davids and Sons, Inc. Landscaping, and has lectured at the University of Ill. and Triton College. Mr. Davids innovated many firsts in the village such as the Ice Sculpture Contest, band concerts and new play equipment.

COMMUNITY INVOLVEMENTS

Chairman Evergreen Park, Park Board
Park Board member, 10 years
Board member Evergreen Park Chamber of Commerce
Chairman Cleanup and Fixup Committees that were nationally recognized with Awards
Mission Chairman, Church School Teacher Christian Reformed Church
Member Regular Republican Party

Candidate for Village President Mayor in 1973.

American Association
of Nurserymen

This Letter issued to   CLARENCE DAVIDS, SR.

for participation in

SEMINAR II
Nursery Management

Conducted July 25-30, 1976 by Syracuse University Faculty
at Colorado State University, Ft. Collins, Colorado

Executive Vice President   *Academic Director*

University College
of Syracuse University

This certifies that

CLARENCE DAVIDS, SR.

has participated in the

A.A.N. Nursery Management Seminar

Conducted July 27 - August 1, 1975 by University College in cooperation with the
American Association of Nurserymen.

Eric Lawson
Academic Director

Frank E. Funk
Dean, University College

Extended education certificates
received in 1975 and 1976.

Certificate from Triton College
received May 21, 1976 for teaching landscape design.

Received Certficate as Registered Landscape Architect from the State of Illinois through the grandfather clause in 1997.

40th Anniversary of Clarence Davids & Co Corporation at the branch office in Naperville, Illinois.

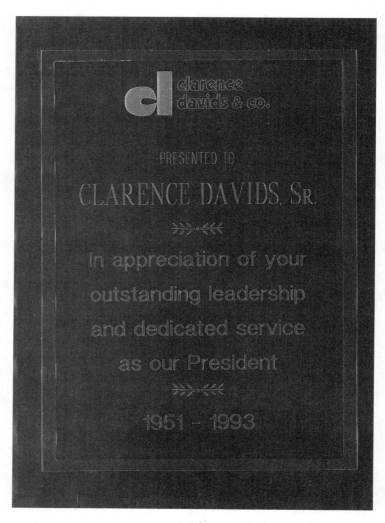

Award given as President and owner of
Clarence Davids Sr. and Co. in 1993.

Clarence Davids Sr. wins John Hyman Award

The Cosmopolitan Chamber of Commerce of Chicago recently presented the **JOHN HYMAN AWARD** to Clarence Davids, Sr., chairman of Clarence Davids and Company. For the past year Mr. Davids has been mentor to minority landscaper, Thumbs Up Lawn Care, owned by Keith Miller. The John Hyman Award was created twenty years ago in honor of a Turner Construction Company executive who devoted most of his personal time to assisting struggling minority contractors to improve their management and marketing capabilities.

Clarence Davids, Sr.
Founder and Chairman of Clarence Davids & Co.

Hyman Award Received October 4, 1996.

THE JOHN HYMAN AWARD
Presented To
CLARENCE DAVIDS
CLARENCE DAVIDS AND COMPANY
In recognition of his consistent and
exemplary record of assistance to
minority construction businesses
October 4, 1996

Plaque received for minority mentoring
from the City of Chicago on October 4, 1996.

Dedication plaque inside Groot Hall,
Clarence Davids Sr. Business Center.

Dedication of the Clarence Davids Sr. Business Center.
A.J. Anglin, Joyce, Clarence, Bill Weidenaar, John Kooyenga

TRINITY

CHRISTIAN COLLEGE

*Clarence Davids and
Joyce Vander Bent Davids
Business Scholarship*

TRINITY

CHRISTIAN COLLEGE

*Jospehine Davids
Memorial Scholarship*

Business Award for eight scholarships given each year.

Chapter Thirteen

A Partnership

As the partnership began, I was working for the company, but I knew that my true talents were not being utilized. Shoveling and wheeling dirt around was a far cry from what I had learned to do in the service.

One day I mentioned to my new partner, "You know, George, I don't mind working as a laborer, but sometimes I feel like a mule and know that I can be more of an asset to this company in other ways."

"What ways are those, Clarence?" he asked.

I did not want to come across as a complainer or like a know-it-all, but I had to speak my piece. As frustrated as I quickly was becoming, I knew that speaking boldly about my feelings was needed. "I can run any piece of equipment there is. If we had some equipment our work would really progress, and I need the chance to do it."

George was a good landscaper and had worked the business for years. I respected him for this. The following day, he came to me and mentioned that Ford had a new tractor out, and it was a loader with no down pressure. He then went on to tell me that he couldn't afford to buy one. I encouraged him to have the Ford salesman come over and talk to us and perhaps even demonstrate it for us.

George and I went together to the Ford tractor dealer, and the salesman took us to lunch. He explained all the features, warranties, and finally mentioned the price. George immediately balked at what they were asking for it and told the salesman and I that he could never afford to buy one.

As we left the dealership, I knew in my heart that George and I had come to a crossroads. Driving back to our work area, I told him that I could buy the tractor myself. I then had an idea that meant the dissolution of our partnership.

"I'll tell you what, George. I'll buy the tractor, using my own money. You can hire me and pay me an hourly wage for my time spent on the machine doing work for you. I'll let you know how much an hour I will charge you."

George agreed to hire me by the hour, but it was only a day or so later that I realized our overall arrangement and partnership had become impotent and useless.

I approached him and said, "George, we ought to end this thing right now. We obviously don't need each other."

"You're right," he replied. "It's a good idea to split up."

Turf Builders—Steps to Success:

- Never let your frustrations build up. Work them out and speak them out before you blow it.
- Always be prepared to move ahead rather than stand still. Never let a hurdle to cross become a stumbling block. Jump it and move on to success.
- Relational integrity is paramount in successful living.

Chapter Fourteen

Working the Business

It was time to start on my own, and the thrill of my lifetime was just beginning: I would be in business for myself. It was also pretty scary.

The first truck I bought was a brand-new Ford dump truck. I did my best not to go into debt, so I made sure that I borrowed only a small portion for this vehicle. My dad never went in debt for anything. He even bought our homes with cash, so I suppose this has been a good trait that I have inherited from him.

The new truck had a Heil dump body on it, and I knew it was a good one because it was the same kind of dump body Dad used in his business. I soon had that truck working all day and sometimes into the night. We hauled tons and tons of dirt with it. The topsoil that I delivered was guaranteed to be the best. If the customer did not like it, he did not have to pay for it, or I would bring him another load free of charge.

All of my material was purchased from other Dutch-men who were in the business of stripping the dirt off the land before the excavating was done for building sites. It worked out very good for all of us.

Not only would they scrape the surface dirt off, they also would pulverize and grind it as well, so this left me with the finest black dirt in town. Jo took phone calls all day long for topsoil orders. We had truly become a family business.

Jo worked as diligently as I did to see that we succeeded. She was my accountant and secretary as I spent long hours working just as my dad did before me.

I stood on my guarantees. If anyone complained about the dirt that I delivered, I was right there to check out the dirt and make things right. I never hesitated to satisfy the customers, and I know this is partly why I am successful today. The old adage "The customer is always right" can-not be underestimated in any business. It is just good busi-ness to back up your product or work by being willing to take a loss. If you are willing and act on it, then you will never lose in the long run.

Soon after splitting up with George, I learned how to asphalt from my brother-in-law. I was able to put my tractor and other pieces of equipment to good use. I was also able to exercise my talents and skills honed in the Army Air Corps. Soon I had an asphalting branch built into my new business.

Asphalting driveways was a natural for what I was do-ing in landscaping. It went hand-in-hand. When the lawns were cared for, I took careful notice of the condition of each driveway that rimmed the grass, greenery, and gar-den areas. When I found a customer's driveway in bad repair, I could make suggestions on how to improve it. Many times the driveways were in such bad condition that it usually resulted in putting in a new driveway from my asphalt branch.

However, most of my asphalt business came from new construction. When I was first beginning, there were new subdivisions and new homes springing up everywhere. I could not run out of work. All I had to do was be steady at the helm and do what work was in front of me. This is another lesson I learned early in my business, and I carried it all the way through. And that lesson? Never exceed your capacity to deliver an excellent product. Always finish the job at hand before trying to take on any more work.

When George and I broke up our partnership and he went his way and I went mine, I felt like a new man. He had taught me a lot about the business, and I had the energy (plus money in the bank), so it was just a matter of getting the breaks, which I did. Again, like my dad, somebody gave me a job at which I could learn and grow. He taught me the ropes, and I was off and running.

I had left the trailer park and built a small home with an extra garage. I started the business at home, and it was ideal for what I needed. I had a wonderful garage that I had built there. It could hold a couple of trucks, and I could run crews from there. All of our equipment was left at my home for the time being.

We grew again, and the equipment at home was getting to be too much. I had to find other arrangements for that.

One of my very best friends is Marty Ozinga. He owns the bank that I have always used. Without Marty, I never could have grown like I did. He always made sure that the necessary funds were available for me to use for my expansion. Only once did I ever have to put up collateral for a loan. It was my house, and Jo said never again.

Through his trust and confidence in me, I have always had the best of credit ratings, and at times when business got bad, I could count on his bank to shore me up during the weak and lean times.

Marty had a large yard where he kept materials. He also owned a premixed-concrete company. His family owned a coal and oil business, and they kept those materials in this yard too.

He and I had a lot of common interests. Marty was a veteran of the war like myself. He was a combat pilot, and we have grown to love being with one another to share our pasts and our futures. He is also a wonderful Christian brother and serves the Lord like no one I've ever seen. He remains a bright example to everyone who knows him.

One day I asked him, "Marty, what I need is someplace to keep my equipment. I'm growing so fast that I can't keep everything at home anymore."

He then suggested that I get a trailer built for commercial offices and turn it into my administrative office and keep the entire operation in the materials yard. It was like God had orchestrated another miracle. It was just what I needed. Another blessing of being in the Ozinga material yard: the rent was dirt cheap!

The next thing I did was make up some brochures with our services and who we were and mailed them out to certain areas of town. The brochures also added another dimension for our family business; our children were hired to go out and hang brochures on doors in the different neighborhoods.

I began to hire more workers and train them. I passed on what I knew, and I soon had a good crew of hard-working men. We started with one truck and today have dozens more. Each truck is outfitted with all the essential tools for landscaping and gardening: mowers, edgers, clippers, ladders, weeders, seed, fertilizer, spreaders, shovels, rakes, hoes, hoses, etc.

I took a tip from my dad when it came to painting our name on the trucks. Dad always figured that if you presented yourself as a high-class operation, then high-class business would come your way. What he was really trying to say is that if you present yourself as a man, a worker, or a company that strives to do the very best job possible, then you will succeed. For instance, when he first started his garbage business, he did not have "Nick Davids' Garbage Company" painted on the side of his trucks. Instead, he painted, "Nick Davids–Private Scavenger," in very upscale lettering on each door of the trucks. He was always into upgrading the image of his business and trade. I learned this well because I, too, have always liked to present professionalism in whatever I do.

One of the first things I did after leaving the partnership of George was to reassess my estimating and bidding process. He taught me a lot in the business, including how to give estimates for jobs.

George's way of estimating was to go on the site and use what he called his "rule of thumb." He would size things up by saying, "It looks like about a hundred yards of sod over here, and about four yards of this over here, and about six yards of this material there. Yeah, and he wants us to put some trees in too, and I can cut that cost if I put in two-footers instead of four-footers. In a couple of years no one will notice the difference. . . ."

Because I knew there was a better way of doing these particular details of the trade, I changed my ways of estimating when I got out on my own. I began to take courses on how to legitimately estimate jobs. I needed to price everything where the customer gets the best of what I could offer, and at the same time, I would make what I needed and wanted on each job. There was no room for guessing any longer.

I also knew that computers were the way of the future. I inherently knew that someday they would not only be used by large financial institutions—the government and other such entities—but also in every aspect of small businesses as well.

I began to learn about computers as well. Not that I was interested in becoming an operator of one, but I knew that I had to know how they worked because someday I would have employees using them. Most of my studies were done at the Purdue University. To me, this university was the Mecca for what I needed to know.

Computers then were not what they are today. The least you could pay for one was around twenty-five hundred dollars, and it had to be kept in a refrigerated room. They were all big units—nothing small. A Pentium laptop was not even imagined back then by most people. I tried to stay on the cutting edge of the latest technology, and it was all done to improve my potential in business and produce a better product for my clients.

At the university, I also took courses in time study. Here I learned how to correctly time a job. I would take a crew of men to a job site, give them a start, and jot down the time they started. I would then note how long it took to do certain tasks. How much grass was mowed here? How many square feet of this and how long?

I spent many long nights on job sites to perfect this system. It took a lot of time—a lot of extra time—to do time studies. But it paid off.

By the time we finally got our computers up and running, I had all the figures measured and written. All I had to do was give them to our computer person and let him input and convert them for our use in bidding and estimating. I had one of the very best bidding systems in the industry, and my son still uses it today in the business. It appears to be an ageless system, and it is one that I am extremely proud of.

In the beginning, I didn't have a title, such as "landscaper." I, along with every other landscaper in town, was known as a grass cutter. We cut grass and trimmed hedges and sidewalks. Even though I mingled landscape construction into the lawn care, we really didn't distinguish ourselves as anything but "grass cutters." I found myself working night and day just to keep up with everything that had to be done. I was soon burning the candle at both ends.

Turf Builders—Steps to Success:

- Never exceed your capacity to deliver an excellent product, and always finish the job at hand before trying to take on any more work.
- Guesswork will someday create more work and less money.
- Always look for ways to upgrade your presentation and image.

Chapter Fifteen

Expanding the Business

I could not keep up the pace I was going at, and work became my worst enemy. I didn't know how to pace myself. I could not meet payroll and was having to lay people off.

The age thirty-six was a difficult number for our family. My only sister passed away of cancer at that age, and one of my older brothers died of leukemia at thirty-six. This was a time in my life that became difficult as well.

It was at this time that I collapsed both physically and mentally. I checked myself into a private, Christian hospital health ward for treatment. It was a defining time in my life. I did not know how badly I needed someone to intervene in my life and give me direction (along with the treatment). I also needed the rest.

Jo was a jewel to support me at this time. She did what she could to keep the business intact and running. She actually fired all of my employees for not listening to a woman boss. She also learned to drive a car at this time. Necessity is sometimes the best coach to move us into uncharted waters. We did lose a couple of jobs in my absence, but all in all, I believe the Lord had His hands upon us and kept us.

I spent several weeks at the hospital, and I cannot say enough for the care and treatment I received—especially spiritually. At the time, many people did not like to talk about these kind of circumstances because of the shame involved. It was difficult to admit that help was needed. However, we did not hide it. Jo put it on the bulletin at church and asked that we be remembered in prayer.

When I was released, I felt like a new man. I also felt as though I could continue to build, where before I was overwhelmed, confused, and just plain worn out emotionally. This is where I became reborn in Christ Jesus.

It is amazing as I look back and see how the Lord was orchestrating all of the steps in building my business. I had a problem in my business, and He knew everything about it. Not being able to keep employees happy because of the uncertainty of the cash flow was certainly a major problem. I knew that I had to make some changes to avoid collapsing again, and He helped me do that. He put Mrs. Johnson in my path.

Not long after I got back to work, I met this wonderful lady named Mrs. Johnson. I became her gardener. During the wintertime, my landscaping work always took a dive. It is that time of year that grass does not grow, so you cannot mow and trim it. Likewise it is not the time of year to put in most plants. So I took a job working at a gas station to fill in the loss of income. The owner was a Mr. Johnson, and this is how I became acquainted with his wife. She became one of my new landscaping accounts, and we got along terrifically. She was a woman with much

Jewish wisdom about business, so I made a point to listen when she gave advice.

One day she took me aside and challenged me to enlarge my sphere of business As usual, I listened intently as she imparted the wisdom of expanding my field of operations. As she was sharing with me the ideas of branching out, I could see that she was really communicating a need that her whole neighborhood had: they wanted someone trustworthy and steady to maintain their lawns and garden areas.

She suggested that I start a new division in my business that was strictly lawn-care maintenance. I should have two separate crews: one to do the landscaping, and the other to do the lawn maintenance. This made sense to me, and it was like a light bulb went off in my head. *Sure*, I thought, *this is exactly how I can expand the business, and it will take the least amount of effort. It's a natural!*

It was like a miracle happened that day. It seems like as soon as I made the decision to make two branches, everyone in the world was looking for someone to maintain their lawn on a regular basis. Nearly overnight I had more than enough work in both divisions.

Mrs. Johnson continued to help in the process. She went to all her wealthy friends and began letting them know of my lawn-care and maintenance business. Almost overnight my business seemed to take a quantum leap. I had to begin a serious hiring campaign just to keep up with it all because my landscape-construction division was doing more business than usual.

Mrs. Johnson hit the nail on the head. She was right—the timing was perfect to expand the way we did. With this versatility, the whole industry was open to me. Whenever someone who had us maintaining their lawn needed some new landscaping (construction) done, we were ready for it and could do it without missing a beat. I changed our name to Clarence Davids and Sons Landscaping Maintenance Company. Shortly afterward I settled on the business name that we have today: Clarence Davids & Company.

———

One of the first frustrations of this new aspect of business was the competition of bidding. In these smaller residential accounts, landscapers with less overhead could show up and bid lower, so I was losing business. In order to handle this, we just went bigger and found new markets.

We started bidding on larger contracts (ones that the smaller landscapers couldn't do because of the lack of personnel or equipment). We were soon landing the larger commercial, industrial, federal, and state jobs. This is where the money proved to be. Plus we never had much of a problem collecting our pay from these larger accounts.

There is more money to be made in landscape contracting, but the drawback is that it is not consistent. Landscape maintenance is a constant source of income. It seldom wavers, and when it does, it usually is to our benefit because we are adding new accounts all the time.

However, Clarence Davids & Company was the very first company to begin doing landscape maintenance and construction on a contract basis. We were the first to have maintenance routes with genuine, bona fide contracts signed between customer and landscaper.

All of these incidents added up to my becoming the single pioneer of landscape management. I was the first landscaper in Chicago to be known as a landscape manager. This is why I am known as the "grandfather of landscape management."

The expansion just kept going from that point on. We opened another office at Ninety-fifth, off Kedzie Avenue, in

Evergreen Park. We were on our way, and I attribute much success to Mrs. Johnson's tips. My problems of keeping good staff in slow times of the year were solved. I merely added on to my business a service that was needed and wanted.

After several months of operating out Marty Ozinga's material yard, we had grown so much that it was time to move again, and we finally found some offices and space for equipment at Blue Island on the South Side of Chicago. Clarence Davids & Company used this as its base of operation for over thirty years. It was the perfect spot for us.

I lived in Evergreen Park at the time, and Blue Island was close to home also. This meant that it was easier for me to spend more time with my family.

How the move to Blue Island came about is interesting. One of the brothers in our church was a builder who owned a building there. The building came with a large yard in the rear and twice as much room inside than we needed, but at the rate of growth I had been experiencing, I knew that someday we could use it.

Financially there was no way we could afford the huge commercial property that he had up for lease, but in faith I took out a two-year lease. Shortly after I did, my eldest son came to me with some good news. He had heard about another man—a Dutchman—who had two furniture moving trucks. He could not find space to park them. Immediately I tracked down the man and told him of the property and offered to rent out some space to him, and he took me up on the offer.

Then I found another man who had bought some property in Orland Park, which is a little further south than Blue Island. I called him and began querying him about why he had not built on the property yet, and he told me that he did not have the finances to build yet. Then he confided in me that he was presently overcrowded where his business was, and he needed storage room. I offered him a section of my warehouse to store his goods and supplies, and he accepted the offer.

It is amazing how creative one can be when one is not only looking out for one's self, but is doing things that intentionally help others, too. Now I could afford the rent on the property, and I could do a good service for someone in need.

Turf Builders—Steps to Success:

- Never allow personal pride drive you to exhaustion. There is always another day to do what must be done on earth.
- Choose your counselors wisely, but be willing to listen to anyone who may have a word of advice that you may need.
- Timing is everything. Sometimes it is better to wait and evaluate than to rush and become frustrated.
- Find out what is needed and wanted and produce it for or present it to the customer. Filling needs is an honorable way to do business.

Chapter Sixteen

In Business for Yourself

The excitement of owning your own business can sometimes be dampened by human nature. I've never been one to deal very well with procrastination, nor have I ever been a good bill collector.

Probably the most difficult part of owning your own business is collecting money that is owed to you. My wife, Jo, was my accountant at the time, and she was not one to sit still when things got out of kilter with the finances. I would have so much money out and owed to me on jobs, that it was a constant source of stress for all of us.

It was at this time that I took a Dale Carnegie course, and it helped my confidence considerably in confronting human situations. I was blessed to have Jo support and encourage me while I took this training. The nice thing about it was that it became a family affair. My kids were the cheerleaders for me to succeed, and Jo was their coach. It was a great feeling to have her honor me by keeping my children abreast of my progress week by week. At the end of it, not only did my business benefit, but I also did personally as well.

The Carnegie course I took was primarily a course in public speaking. This, above all things, built my confidence in business.

The course was six grueling weeks long. I did not stay at a campus; I attended only on Fridays. They allowed me to fit it into my schedule, and this was why it was possible for me to complete it. Each week we were required to come prepared to give a speech, and these were judged heavily. If one's talk was the best, that person got a pin from Dale Carnegie. Those of us participating came to feel as though we would die for a silly little pin.

I did not get my pin until the last week, and I was ready to give up. Each week I would come home, and my children really got into it with me. They would ask, "Did you get the pin, Dad?"

"No, not this week," I'd reply and almost hang my head.

One week after letting them know that I did not get the pin again, I was told by one of them that it was doubtful that I'd ever get it. This only made me try harder.

Finally, in the last week, I came home wearing the pin. It was a special bonding time for our entire family, and I was so proud to have children that cared so much about what their father was involved in.

During this time, I began to make a practice of taking a day a week to be a bill collector. I learned to switch hats and do something completely different than I was accustomed to doing. I would put on a suit and tie and go see my customers. With difficulty, I collected what was due us for work rendered.

I had to learn how to be the owner of a business, not just a worker. By taking responsibility for the retrieving of money from delinquent accounts, I grew leaps and bounds

Turf Builders—Steps to Success:

- Always know the limitations of those whom you expect to do work for you. If you do, your expectations will never let you down.
- Always treat others as you would expect to be treated yourself.
- Honor your employees, and you will receive double honor back.

Chapter Seventeen

Education and Association

My father was my first educator. I observed him in all his ways of doing business and interacting with people. The Army Air Corps gave me an opportunity to learn valued skills that were honed with on-the-job training. George became my mentor in 1951. While working for him and with him, I began my formal education in the field I was best at. The professors at Purdue University and at the University of Illinois—plus the special seminars and lectures and the Dale Carnegie Course—all added to my knowledge and success in landscape management. However, not enough can be said about hands-on experience in the field.

In the field of landscape management, education became a critical step in the success of my business. I learned things at Purdue University and the University of Illinois that gave me certainty in areas where other landscapers without that knowledge could only take a shaky guess. If there was one true mentor to be named in my life, I would have to say it was the faculty at the U of Illinois who came alongside me. They walked me through many areas of uncertainty until I grasped what they were trying to say to me, and I devoured their teachings.

Not only did I attend seminars and classes at the U of I, but also I would travel as far as California to learn about a new technique, about a new way to fertilize grass, or about planting and caring for plants properly. Some of these instructors were college-level professors. I had much admiration for them, their knowledge, and how they disseminated it to their students. They were not just "book" people. These people were experienced in what they taught.

At these seminars and classes, there would always be those of us who would be so hungry for information that we would barely let the instructors out of our sight. Some of us ended up talking and drinking with them into the wee hours of the night. We would pour drinks and pump them for more insight and more information. Give them some drinks and let them talk. We would sit back and take it all in as if our lives depended on what they were saying.

As I look back in my life, I feel that if I could change anything, it would be the time I spent getting a formal education. I had scorn for education in my youth but I am still learning!

Not that I would trade any amount of book learning for the thrill of having a successful business, mind you, but learning new things has always been a major part of my dreams. These classes and seminars provided me with a slight taste of receiving this kind of education. Not that more education would have made me more successful, but I simply like absorbing knowledge.

Teacher-student interaction is very important. I believe that in order to get the best, well-rounded education, every person needs to have someone who will walk alongside them and mentor or tutor them in practical ways. Getting theoretical information is fun and mentally stimulating, but there is nothing like the excitement of seeing a project go from drawing board to physical manifestation. For me this could not happen in a classroom. It occurred only in the field with sleeves rolled up, hands on the plow, and sweat rolling down my brow.

And chances are, today this type of work experience comes in the presence of a good mentor who is committed to seeing you do the best you can with what you have. Now a special blessing has come my way: I have had the privilege in 1997 and 1998 to act as a mentor in a minority program for landscaping in Chicago.

Every good student or apprentice needs a real human being to walk alongside of him, to give pointers and counsel. It is necessary to sometimes work by trial and error because the mentor has moved off at a distance just to watch. He may want to see which parts of the character will surface when faced with unknowns and uncertainties. But the trial-and-error period is brief because a true mentor will never allow his protégé to flounder too long so as to become discouraged.

Experience is one way to learn the indutry of landscaping. In my day, it was the only way. Sure, I went to school to improve what was already in my heart to do, but I would never have succeeded if I had not had a base of work experience. I have done my best to pass this asset on to my children and to those in my employ and sphere of influence.

Turf Builders—Steps to Success:

- Always do your best to get an education with a good balance of theory and practice.
- Knowledge is useless unless it is shared in a positive manner.
- Today, skipping formal education is comparable to "reinventing the wheel." Take advantage of education while it is offered.

Chapter Eighteen

Who and Where We Are

One of the things I learned from my dad is the importance of pride that one's employees should have for where they work. I found that to develop a dress code for my field employees was a major step to success, like the large sign painted on the side of his truck "Nick Davids—Private Scavenger." Not only did it give each employee a sense of belonging to something bigger than himself, but it also gave the company more of a professional image to the public.

Today the Clarence Davids & Company workforce has shirts imprinted with our logo and name on them. Each outside employee wears the uniform with pride. I discovered that the public, who puts its finances and trust in us, is more confident in our relationship with them when they see employees wearing clean and professional company clothing. When you are in business for yourself, it is critical always to put your best foot forward. Your image could make the difference in getting work and not getting work.

Even though most of the jobs are obtained through a bidding process, the public always will show more leniency and favor to the vendor that displays the greatest amount of professionalism.

Today Clarence Davids & Company has a motto: Nobody Makes You Look Better than Clarence Davids Landscaping. We have become a professional landscape, design, build, and maintenance company. We conduct ourselves in a manner to address all the needs of our customers to the best of our abilities. We believe that God has given us the knowledge to operate the way we do, and we see His hand in our success on a daily basis.

We have been in business for nearly fifty years, and our name is identified with landscaping all over the State of Illinois. We actually do not need to advertise all that much to bring in consistent or new business. People just know us by what we do and by our reputation of excellence.

We like to deliver excellence in everything we do. Sometimes we may find it beneficial to add another truck and some more staff, but not as frequently as in the beginning. We are sort of a controlled-growth company, and that is how we have chosen to do things. Presently my son Bill, who is now the owner, runs the business. We have a fleet of 75 trucks on the road.

In 1985 we opened a branch facility on a ten-acre site in Plainfield, located near Naperville, Illinois. In 1993 a second branch was opened on a twenty-acre site in northwest suburban Ingleside near Gurnee, Illinois. Our specialties have become landscape management, design/build landscape construction, installation, and full lawn-care fertilization programs.

Clarence Davids & Company has left the Blue Island facility and now has its own forty acres in the Matteson, Illinois, area. Here there is ample space to stock materials, maintain equipment, and administrate the business.

We now operate in three different states: Illinois, Wisconsin, and Indiana.

Clarence Davids & Company is environmentally conscious of its clients' needs. We maintain a separate in-house lawn-care department with the State of Illinois, certified and licensed, lawn-care pesticide applicators and operators. The company practices Integrate Pest Management (IPM), including environmentally friendly products to help protect our environment. The company also uses composting of grass clippings to be utilized as a soil amendment, which conserves space in the Chicago-area landfills.

The company takes great pride in maintaining high standards in all aspects of business. Our labor force consists of well-trained people in each skill required to maintain and/ or landscape any property. Our training programs coincide with our safety programs.

Behind the scenes, keeping equipment running and looking attractive, is a full-service team of mechanics in three offices, and our professional office staff is dedicated to an excellent standard of customer service.

Clarence Davids & Company has been honored with over 100 national, state, and local awards for its landscape excellence.

As for the future of the company, I would like to see the company extend itself to doing pools and fountains. This is the way of the future for landscape contracting. This could be a new division within the company. It is what the contemporary customer is asking for, so I hope that the decision is made to add it soon.

My advice for anyone who is starting out in business for themselves is to, first and foremost, have their priorities in place. The first thing you must have is an absolute trust in the Lord Jesus to pull you through every situation.

I know there are people out there who appear to be succeeding, and they don't know God or respect Him. But in my estimation as a Christian, this is only an illusion. I can only go back to Psalm 73 where Asaph, as a believer, had gotten very discouraged about his earthly condition. He saw the wicked prosper, and he saw the righteous going without. He said that his feet almost slipped because of this, but then he came to his senses and saw that the end of every endeavor, including life on earth, must be settled with God. And His final word assures the destruction of the wicked. So, I can conclude only that their success is like a vapor—very temporal, to say the least.

Turf Builders—Steps to Success:

- The public will always lean toward and favor the vendor that displays the greatest amount of professionalism.
- Never forsake the personal touch for the sake of expansion. To do so only weakens your purpose, your dream, and your success.
- Follow the Lord in all that you do, and He will establish your ways.

Chapter Nineteen

The Association

The Illinois Landscape Contractors Association (ILCA) was formed in 1959. It has been one of my life accomplishments of which I am the most proud. No business is without its headaches and problems. For a new businessperson to think he or she will escape unscathed on the way to the top of the success ladder is naïve at best. I could see problems developing not only in my company, but also in other landscape businesses I was familiar with. There were no standards that we could agree upon. There were no ethical principles with which we could protect ourselves. Landscapers were cutting each other's throats through unethical bidding, stealing jobs from one another, and doing work that was shoddy, thereby giving all landscapers a bad name. Something had to be done to make us accountable to one another. No one else could police us but ourselves.

One day I had a thought. *Why not start an association of landscapers so we can all have some rules of competition and work ethics? Why not get all of us together so we can help edu-cate and support one another?* It was an interesting thought, and when I mentioned it to four other active landscapers in the area, they became as excited as I was about it.

We recognized the need for a sincere commitment to our clients, and by joining ourselves together in a professional fraternity, we knew we had touched on what had been needed for years: accountability, standards of operation, respect, and trust.

The idea behind the ILCA was to serve as a forum for the exchange of ideas among landscape contractors, to carry out a broad-scale program of practical instruction, to create a greater degree of public appreciation, and to encourage a high code of professional ethics and workmanship among us.

ILCA began as the Chicago Metro Landscaping Association. However, in short order we could see that this focus was too narrow for what we were trying to accomplish. Since we were trying to get every landscaper in the state to participate, we changed the name to embrace every landscaper in Illinois.

In the beginning the meetings were interesting to say the least. Many times we would almost have brawls between rival landscapers. The solid purposes of the association, though, always came through. When differences and old problems arose, we were able to sort them out to everyone's satisfaction and get on with moving in the direction to grow and become what we have become today—leaders in the field of landscape management.

It is an interesting thing to see how God puts Christians right in the middle of certain groups of people. I had no idea that by forming an association of landscapers, it would lead to witnessing for the Lord.

Some of the men who belonged to ILCA at the time were Christian men. There were times when I had opportunities to share God's goodness with the unbelievers who were members.

One member I know of was an atheist and made no bones about how proud he was of it. He and I went back many years, and we were the best of friends, and I knew that he did not believe there was a God.

One weekend, several members of ILCA, including the executive director of our organization who was a strong Christian as well, were attending classes at the University of Indiana. My friend ended up as one of the other three men in my sleeping quarters. One evening we talked into the night about landscaping, our families, and our businesses, and anything and everything. Eventually the subject of religion had to come around, with Christians and an atheist in the same room.

The executive director began to speak to him about his eternal destination. He was right up-front when he said, "If you were to die tonight, where would you go?"

It seemed like it was God speaking out from heaven. It was two o'clock in the morning, it was dark, and the whole room seemed like a chamber before the throne room of the Father in heaven.

Speaking low and softly, he continued, "Friend, I know you are a nonbeliever; you keep saying it. You are proud because you don't believe in God. I was just wondering because I'm concerned. If you were to die tonight, where would you end up? Do you know whether you would go to heaven or hell?"

We could hear our friend almost choking as he lay in the still darkness. He took a long time in answering the question, but finally he said, "I would hope that I would go to heaven."

"Then you have to live your life according to God's ways."

I know the executive director's words penetrated deep into his heart that evening, and I was extremely proud to be a part of an organization in which this kind of ministry could happen.

I was at this friend's bedside when he died while in a coma some years later. I know that his spirit heard me praying for him as he lay there unconscious, and I hope that someday he and I will meet in heaven. Only God knows at this point.

My Christianity took a new turn at this point through joining the World Home Bible League. Not long after my breakdown, John Davids, my nephew, who was a member of the League, called me and told me that they were short-handed and really needed some help. I didn't know enough about the Bible League at this point, but I was interested and so became involved with his wonderful organization that distributes Bibles all over the world.

It was at this same time I was also asked to be a Sunday school teacher, and I replied, "You have the wrong man." The elders asking then responded with "No, we prayerfully chose your name and are sure you can do this." I didn't know how to turn them away, so I accepted.

I became a Sunday school teacher for seventeen years at my church. This contributed to my interest in evangelism. At the time, I was also serving as the head of the evangelism committee in our church, which led to my attending the Bible League meeting.

I was involved with the World Home Bible League at the same time I was with ILCA. Consequently, I had access to Bibles that I could give to those to whom I ministered. It was a good set of circumstances that the Lord had placed me in.

One of the primary purposes of forming the Illinois Landscape Contractors Association was to take the stigma out of our work.

We were tired of being looked at as a bunch of sodbusters, running around cutting grass for a living. We knew we had a specialized industry, and it took know-how, experience, education, and stamina to do what we did. We set out to let the community and world know that we were professionals in our field.

We organized seminars and workshops to educate ourselves on how to become more professional. We took men who did not even know how to keep their records and books straight and taught them how to dress like professionals, talk like professionals, and to do business with integrity and a degree of professionalism that everyone in ILCA took pride in.

It was during this time that I ventured out and took the Dale Carnegie Course. What a course! I knew that I lacked in the area of selling my business and products to the customer. I also knew that most of the others in ILCA lacked it too, so I was going to kill two birds with one stone. First, Clarence Davids & Company needed for me to become an expert in the area of sales. And second, I could then take what I learned at Dale Carnegie back to ILCA and help others become better at sales too.

The course also became a vital asset when the following year I ran for mayor in Evergreen Park. After the course, my speaking abilities were much greater, and I could hold my own in political debates. That was an experience of a lifetime, even though I lost the election.

During the voting, I panicked and realized that being mayor was too much pressure. I prayed alone and asked God to help me lose the election. I did lose, and I am so glad that it went that way. If I had become mayor, my whole life would have turned out much differently.

Today there are some national organizations which we are involved with. One is PGMS, Professional Grounds Management Society. I was privileged to be President of this group in 1986. ALCA, Associated Contractors of America is another.

One meeting that ties these groups together is the GIE Convention; Green Industry Expo. This one is held in November in Baltimore, Maryland this year (1999). This cooperative effort also includes PLACCA.

The sod busters and grass cutters have come a long way into high tech professional organizations.

Turf Builders—Steps to Success:

- It is always to your advantage to be accountable to something bigger than yourself.
- Allow the Lord to place you in circles of the unfamiliar so that you may serve as His ambassador, and you will not fail.
- Learn the art of communication. In business it is everything.

Chapter Twenty

Family and Business

Jo and I were wed in a small Christian Reformed Church ceremony. Our marriage began as a partnership in business, in church, and then with our children. I learned that running a business and raising a family were like doing a balancing act. I loved working and I loved my family, and finding the right medium was always a challenge that I enjoyed.

Jo and I had four children together, and they became my priority. I knew that if I neglected my family because of business matters, then I was like the man spoken of by Jesus in Matthew 16:26: "For what will a man be profited, if he gains the whole world, and forfeits his soul?" I have always had a fear of the Lord when it comes to priorities.

However, it was not an easy task. With the "Davids drive" that I inherited from my dad, I knew I was prone to putting the business first and making up excuses why the family had to take second place.

At times I found myself wrestling with choices. I found myself justifying. I could say if I put in this extra time on a job or training workers or this or that, then my family will have more wealth, more vacations, more benefits. But I thank the Lord that He seemed always to direct my mind back to what was important. Wealth, vacations, and benefits were not what God was interested in. He was interested in my family and how I would care for them in the ways that meant the most. This always, always, always meant spending good, quality time. It never meant *not* seeing them in return for giving them "things" in the short time that I made for them.

One of the ways I made time for my family was by making the leap from field manager to boss. Instead of getting in a truck to go with a crew, I sent the trucks out on their own and told them I would be by sometime to see if they needed anything from me. I began to delegate my field management responsibilities over to certain men on whom I knew I could count to the get the job done—and to supervise as well.

I trained every man to be courteous to the customer . . . no matter what! I emphasized how important cleanliness is, ensuring that they were cleaning up after themselves. I hardly ever got any complaints.

By doing these actions, I worked myself out of a job of having to be out on trucks or job sites all the time. The only thing the crews needed from me was to estimate jobs and to collect money. I then could spend more time at my office, which was in my home when my children were small.

I know of some small-business owners who worked out of their homes and still find no time to spend with their family (probably making some of the same excuses I mentioned before). It takes intentional decisions to schedule out work and participate with your children.

Participate is the key word.

When I became the owner, not the supervisor, I could participate with the kids and my wife in different aspects of their activities. At times, I took one of our pickup trucks and threw some hay in it. Then I would take my kids and their friends on a hayride. If they had teacher's conferences, Jo and I could both go. PTA meetings and extracurricular activities I always attended in lieu of working. During the winters, when work slowed down, I would spend a lot of time ice skating with them. Later, we got involved with horses and horse shows. It was great fun and a bonding experience for everyone in the family.

Another aspect of quality time, and the most important, was our church life and the development of our Christian walks. In trying to join the church, the pastor refused to meet with us during the day during our free time. I was working evenings and he would not change his agenda for us, which made me angry enough to look elsewhere for a fellowship to attend. I left the Christian Reformed Church and found a small Bible church that seemed to be a good place to attend. I made a good choice.

It was like a breath of fresh air to be in the midst of a church service in which people were being saved at every service. The preacher never failed to give an altar call, and people responded. We were being spiritually fed like never before.

Our children loved going to church and loved the Christian life. When we moved to Evergreen Park, I wanted my two children baptized. So Jo and I made professions of faith together and rejoined the Christian Reformed Church and attended the church in Evergreen Park.

The children also liked our business. From a very young age, each one wanted to be a part of the business in certain ways. They developed work ethics similar to the ones my dad and I developed over the years. They watched both of us conduct good business and followed suit. We were definitely role models for them. Today my children are in business for themselves. They have a strong, competitive drive for excellence and to get ahead.

I was married to Jo for almost forty-five years before she passed on to be with the Lord in 1991. It was a devastating loss. The breast cancer she contracted was deadly, and I could support her only in prayers and by taking care of her needs to keep her as comfortable as possible. When she finally went into the hospital the last time, the Lord was merciful and did not let her suffer long. She died within twelve hours of the final stay. My children were present at her death. We held hands around the bed as she breathed her last breath.

When Jo passed away, I gave two sets of Suzuki bells to the local Christian school in her memory. Two granddaughters (along with others) played the bells for grandparents day. I had planned to remain anonymous about any gifts like this, but it didn't happen that way.

My very special gift in 1992 to Trinity Christian College in her memory was money designated to begin a Business Scholarship Fund for men and women. In the past eight years, we have been able to give four scholarships per year to Trinity. Recently I was able also to establish a fund in my name too. What better way is there to spend money than to use it to promote Christian businessmen and women to be "in the world but not of it"?

After Jo's death, I was like a fish out of water. Having a partner in any relationship for forty-five years will definitely make a mark on your soul. Death of a spouse at any age is so difficult. However, I felt such thankfulness for our many years of happiness. I could not become bitter at God when He had allowed us forty-five years together. Many people do not get this blessing. I felt I had to get on with my life.

Turf Builders—Steps to Success:

- Learn to delegate, as a priority action, when beginning any new activity. Always have the attitude of desire to work yourself out of a job.
- It takes intentional decisions to schedule out work and schedule *in* your family.
- Participation with children is much more beneficial and remunerative than giving them your earnings. Time is worth more than money any day.
- Success in business is only half attained when the spouse is not involved or interested.

Chapter Twenty-one

A New Marriage:
The Second Chapter Begins

I met Joyce only four months after Jo died. Some mutual friends were camping on Lake Michigan and had invited me over. Joyce happened to be visiting. She had been coming to that same lake for a getaway since her husband passed away some four years previously. I had been considering buying a bike, so I rented one and rode along the lake and ended up at their site.

After the introductions, we talked about a lot of things and then the subject came up of the recent loss of my wife. To my surprise she told me that she also was widowed. I could not help myself; I began to cry and I said to her, "But, you're so young. You must have children."

Later she told me that it was this indication of kindness that attracted me to her. She was so impressed that I could cry over someone else's loss. Almost immediately I, too, recognized that we had an affinity for each other, but marriage was far from our thoughts.

131

Our conversation was interesting, and later that evening before leaving, I asked her if she and her children (ages thirteen, fifteen and eighteen) would like to take a boat ride with me the following day. Later, I understand, her conversation with her son went like this:

"I met a man at the beach today with our friends, and he asked if we'd like to go out on a boat in the morning."

"Well, what did you say?" he asked.

"I said no."

"How come you said no? How many people have asked us out on a boat this summer?"

"Well . . . none."

He then said, "I think you should go, and I'll go with you, Mom."

Well, she ended up coming with me, and he put on quite a water-skiing exhibition for us. I was certainly impressed.

A couple of weeks later, I called her and asked her if she would like to have dinner with me, and she turned me down. She said she was too busy.

Not to be thwarted in my efforts, I maintained the "Davids perseverance" and called her again. Once again she told me that she was too busy. The third time was a charm, though . . . and she finally accepted to go to dinner.

We saw each other for several months, and at the time, I was having a terrible time with glaucoma. I was nearly blind and had to have a lot of doctoring. I was using eye drops and whatever else the doctors were giving me for medication. It was a traumatic time for me. People were driving me around and taking care of me. Even Joyce did some driving for me. She now tells me that I was driving like an "old duffer."

Here again, God intervened and performed a miracle in my life. I went for cataract surgery and my eyes were almost 100 percent corrected. I now have twenty-twenty vision with a lens implant.

Joyce was one of my drivers, and it was during this time that we really got to know each other. They say that when you meet later in life, you just know wheather you can make a marriage or not. A lot of people do not go together for very long in late-life romances. We dated and courted for nearly eleven months before getting married.

One great fear Joyce had was that of losing me to death. She did not want to have a short marriage, and with the disparity in our ages, it kept her at arm's length when it came to wedding commitments.

During the eleven months, I proposed to Joyce several times. (When it comes to romance, I am not a slackard.) At the end of our courtship, Joyce felt very courted and honored that I would be so attentive to her. But I knew this was right and that God had His hand in it. I was going to see to it that I did my part to be obedient to what His plans were.

Our wedding was wonderful. A very small wedding was in my plans, but we had over three hundred people invited. It was a wonderful celebration party for everyone.

Joyce told me that she had always said that if she ever got married again, it was going to be a party. And a party we did have. The ceremony was twenty minutes long, and we had beautiful music. Joyce's daughter Rhonda and her sister, Mary, stood up with her, and my son Bill and one of my grandsons Jason stood up with me. Joyce's sons, Joel and Phillip, and two more of my grandsons—John and Jason—ushered. The reception was an open house and dinner.

Joyce and I spent fifteen days honeymooning in Hawaii. It was a special time of getting to know one another. We took a cruise to all the islands and spent one weekend at the Hilton Hawaiian Village in Honolulu.

Several things happened to me shortly after marrying Joyce. I discovered that she was very active in different functions that were foreign to me. First of all, she introduced me to the world of working with mentally impaired people. It was almost as though God inserted a few new brain cells in my head. I suddenly began to look at the mentally impaired with new eyes and had a new level of compassion for them.

When I was young, the handicapped were not treated as they are today. If someone in the Dutch community had a family member that was mentally or physically challenged, they would basically lock them away in their house, and the outside world would never see them again. This was the way to avoid embarrassment and to limit the care of these poor individuals.

Joyce, on the other hand, reaches out and helps educate them. With my new eyes and attitude, I became her helper.

Our church, the Niekerk Christian Reformed Church, in Holland, Michigan, has a special program that Joyce and I work with in donating time. In the summer we have a summer Bible club for mentally impaired adults.

Joyce was a library aide, and after her first husband died, she gave up library work to become the director of a Christian preschool program for five years.

Joyce has a musical bent that I admire immensely. She was a music minor at Calvin College and plays the clarinet, piano, and organ. She loves to sing in the choir. This was the next "stretch" for me. She coaxed me into developing my singing skills.

I had not really sang since the time when I was singing with the other GIs in the All-Girl's Orchestra. However, when Joyce heard me singing alongside her in church, she recognized (through my somewhat loud dirge) some hidden talent.

I was surprised to receive a Christmas present of voice lessons from her. She had me enrolled in voice lessons with a local, retired Christian choir teacher, and lo and behold, I was told that I have a very rare tenor voice. Now I enjoy singing and do it as often as I can. It is good to do something like this and not be embarrassed. Now instead of joyful noise, I have even learned to read music, and my appreciation for the whole subject has grown a lot. We attend as many concerts as she can find.

Joyce and I now both sing in the church choir, and we sing together at home. We have even performed duets in a mission church. This is something I never dreamed was possible for me.

Jo and Joyce have both helped me through things that I could never have tackled on my own. I am deeply thankful that the Lord put them both in my life.

In the matter of God's helpmates I think Proverbs 31:10 best spells it out for me: "An excellent wife, who can find? For her worth is far above jewels." God has been so good to have placed such wonderful women in my life.

Meeting Joyce has been a highlight of my life, and I am now enjoying "the second chapter" of my life. A friend, who is a songwriter, wrote a special song for us after learning about how we met. I would like to share some of the lyrics with you.

Well, I remember when he stopped me,
        I was riding on my bike,
        "Come along and get some pizza
        I know I've some you'll like."
Well, I don't care for pizza
        It's not my favorite in the world,
        "But if you don't like pizza,"
        "Maybe I can convince you
        To eat my crazy bread."
I don't like that crazy bread
        It's not my favorite in the world.
        "If you don't like crazy bread,

You silly, awful brute,
    Maybe I can convince you to try a little fruit."
Well, fruit, it does taste good to me,
    It's my favorite in the world,
    I discovered it was nothing compared to the girl.
    "I'll take somebody skiing,"
    That's what I said next day.
    "Glad for someone to go with me,
    I've got the boat not far away."
She said she didn't want to go,
    I was broken-hearted then.
    Things don't always go the way you think they will.
    I was overjoyed when I saw her the next day,
    She said she didn't want to ski
    Really cannot tell what it was that
    Changed her mind that day,
    I really think she kind of liked the man.
And now we've been together
    All these six delightful years.
    The good times and the bad times
    And the smiling and the tears.
    I still don't like the pizza,
    It's not my favorite in the world,
    But I know she likes the man she's with,
    And I sure do like the girl.

                        —Ken Medema

Turf Builders—Steps to Success:

- Your spouse is your first ministry—this person will still be living with you after all the children are gone.
- Marriage is a spiritual, emotional, and material oneness. It cannot be separated out.
- Be willing to leave your comfort zone.

Chapter Twenty-two

Blended Family

J oyce and I have developed a big heart for stepfamilies, or better known these days as "blended families." We have this burden because we are walking the walk and living this ministry for ourselves.

From the time we were married the dynamics unique only to families with stepchildren, step fathers and stepmothers came alive to us. Many blended families are a result of divorce and remarriage, but many are from the tragedy of death. Ours was the latter on both sides. Joyce had lost a husband, and I had lost Jo, and here we were mending our lives together in a new family structure.

Grief is a lump in the throat we learn to live with every day for the rest of our lives. When a tragedy strikes a family, no one is the same ever again. Every relationship has to be worked on forever after a loss in order to survive again as a loving family.

Children involved in a family loss face many of the same questions about the future. One of the prevailing thoughts among them is, *Are we still a family?*

Yes, we have learned that we are still a family. However, our lives become like a book when the second marriage begins, and we are now beginning chapter two. Chapter one is over, and yet at the same time, it is not over. We still live with the old and the new every day.

It has not been easy. We enrolled for family counseling almost immediately upon discovering that the "blending" was not going to be easy. We had this counseling for more than three years, and it has been exactly what the Lord meant for us to do to try to meld ourselves into the family unit that He desires. We cannot say enough for Christian counseling when it comes to constructing new families from the broken pieces left by the death of a spouse.

In our marriage, Joyce and I have determined to pray for all of our children each day. This keeps us mindful of the need that is always there for us to be attentive to their needs—especially the spiritual ones.

With so many children involved on both sides, the relationships begin to get complicated—their pain is always our pain. And when we see other families in the "blending process" our hearts go out them. We understand where they are, and identification with them is key to being able to minister God's love to them in a genuine way.

There are many questions that arise when families start to blend, and they are indicative of the challenges these families deal with on a daily basis. Questions, such as: Can children ever fully accept a second spouse? Does the step-parent have authority in the home? (The public image of a stepfather, for example, is disastrous; so how do we cope with that?) Does the second wife or husband have the needed value from the children to make a balanced family and home? How do we learn to honor a second husband or wife in a blended family scene? How do we organize holiday visitations and celebrations? What about birthdays and even anniversaries of the first marriage (if we are widowed)? How do we comfortably blend two families—families who have been living in different camps, with different rules, and different expectations of each other? These "camps" are not intentional divisions. They are merely where each family has been living with their particular interests that have been set in place over the years. These interests, etc., may not agree with, or align to, the interests of the second family that is now involved with them, so this creates some challenging problems for everyone.

Questions such as these can sometimes be pressing, and they do demand answers for each family member who wants to find a comfortable balance. Joyce and I have done several things to try to capture that balance. For example, we have adopted a practice when it comes to a deceased spouse's birthday, or an anniversary of some kind. We try to honor the first spouse on these occasions by pledging or making donations in their remembrance to our favorite charities. This feels good and works fine for us.

I mentioned earlier that we pray for our children. One particular area of prayer is that our children will not be bitter toward God for not helping heal a spouse who has had a terminal illness. God can take a lot of undue blame when He chooses not to heal a mate. Addressing all the issues surrounding this is to have wisdom.

It is a terrible thing to lose a mother or father. And if the grieving process for the children is interrupted by the introduction of a second spouse, more conflict areas can be created for the new marriage. Much prayer, asking for God's divine guidance in these matters, is a wise thing to do.

What to do with family and personal possessions brings to the surface another type of conflict. With that comes an entirely new set of questions, such as: Who owns the things that are left from the first marriage? Or, What do the parents owe their children—if anything?

I know that many people who are in the process of putting a blended family together may ask themselves, *Is marriage a second time worth all this trouble?* Sadly, there are many people (Joyce and I have met some) who realize the problems I just mentioned and choose not to remarry. Many of our older adults are living together without marriage. They feel there are just too many things to work out to make it work, but we have found it be very rewarding, and we love to encourage others to step out in faith and find the happiness that Joyce and I now have.

Many people we meet simply do not want to share anything with a new spouse. For these people not to remarry because they are unwilling to share the fruit of their lives is sad. Our hearts go out to those who are burdened with this attitude, and we pray and encourage these people as often as we can. Marriage is a spiritual, emotional, and material oneness that Joyce and I are blessed to realize. Most importantly, we know (and remind each other often) that everything belongs to God, and we have never seen anyone take with him what he has when this life is over.

We appreciate and understand the loneliness of widowed people. We also understand the loneliness that can happen in a second marriage. There is a saying that "it sometimes feels lonely in the midst of a crowd," and I know what this means now. When we first got married, Joyce and I both lost many good friends. We have had many, many changes in friendships, and this is not easy. But in the long run, it has been more than worth it to blend our lives as we have.

We have heard so much pain from so many on these issues surrounding widowed and stepfamilies. Over the last few years, we have also met some very special people who have encouraged us with kind words and support. In light of that, we feel it only seems appropriate to turn and give out some of what we have received. Joyce and I both love the encouraging words of the prophet Jeremiah: "'For I know the plans that I have for you,' declares the Lord, 'plans to prosper you and not to harm you, plans to give you hope and a future'" (29:11).

We have often heard (and read) the comment, "Many marry a second time for companionship." Actually, we have never met one person who fits into that category. Second marriages are as much for love as the first ones—and sometimes more! If they were based only on filling a need for a companion, how could they ever survive so much added adversity?

In the blending of our lives and families, Joyce and I are constantly reminded of the lyrics from one of our favorite verses, "For such a time as this I was placed upon earth to hear the voice of God, and to do His will . . . ." (Book of Esther 4:14b).

Turf Builder—Steps to Success:

- What we believe to be our greatest weakness, usually results in our greatest strength if we abide in God's will. When I am weak, He is strong!
- Marriage is two people coming together out of love, and this forms the best kind of partnership.
- A marriage that invites God to be a three-way partner will always succeed:

Two are better than one because they have a good return for their labor, for if either of them falls, the one will lift up his companion. But woe to the one who falls when there is not another to lift him up. Furthermore, if two lie down together they keep warm, but how can one be warm alone? And if one can overpower him who is alone, two can resist him. A cord of three strands is not quickly torn apart (Eccles.) 4:9–12.

- Encouragement—whether giving it or receiving it—is a wonderful thing!

Chapter Twenty-three

Trinity College:
What Do You Need?

Forty some years ago, a school was formed in Palos Heights, Illinois. It was christened Trinity Christian College. I became involved with its inception and have been an avid supporter of the school from day one.

I had served as the adjunct professor in landscape gardening and design at Triton College. I also served as an instructor of professional turf management and landscape at Chicago State University, so my interest in advanced education was a perfect foundation for getting involved with the founding of a Christian College.

Not only was I able to sit on the board and offer my landscaping expertise in designing and caring for the campus, but I also have been able to offer my services to an instructor in the business department. I have watched Groot Hall—the business school department of Trinity—grow in activity every year and have been personally blessed to be a part of that.

My good friend John Kooyenga has been a special blessing to me. He is the head of business department at the school
and has been a strong encourager for me to finally write this
book. In my special affinity for Trinity Christian College, I
have found a channel through which to pour what God has
blessed me with. I believe in my heart that He is pleased too.

My intention has never been to receive any glory for
my service; it is all the Lord's. But probably my proudest
moment was when the Trinity Christian College Business
Department was named after me on May 8, 1998.

In a book such as this, it is difficult for the author to
speak of his own achievements or activities where others
were helped. To share with you, the reader, how much I
love and desire to support this school, I have asked Mr.
Kooyenga to share his views of my relationship with Trinity Christian College. He writes:

"It was in the mid-1980s, when Clarence Davids was
President of Christians for the Advancement of Business
Leadership Education (CABLE), that we began working together. CABLE was an auxiliary support organization for
the business department of Trinity Christian College. Mem-
bership dues provided financial scholarships for business
students, and the business owners provided role models
for students enrolled in the business program.

"Through the ensuing years, I have had the pleasure of
having many conversations with Clarence, and it has
become apparent that his relationship with Trinity Christian College goes back to the very first days of the college—
the late 1950s. In one of these conversations, he shared
with me that the magnificent evergreen tree that resides in
the area between the dining hall and the administration
building was one of the first landscaping services that he
provided to the college. In many ways, that beautiful ever-

green tree and its splendor, symbolize the relationship that Clarence has had with the college in the last forty years.

"I would imagine that, when planted, it was maybe four to five feet tall and perhaps three to four feet across the bottom. This regal twenty-foot evergreen tree now towers over the roof of the dining hall and probably measures more than twelve feet at the bottom. On the coldest of winter days, with snow accumulating on the ground, it provides the natural warmth and beauty that only an evergreen tree can provide. In July and August, when both the temperature and humidity are above 90, the same beautifully formed evergreen tree, provides the cooling shade needed in the heat of the afternoon.

"From his original role as a landscaping contractor providing services to a client, Clarence's role in the life of the Trinity Christian College, and particularly the business department, has grown in height, breath, splendor and beauty over the last forty years. He has been elected to and served on the board of trustees on several occasions. He also has faithfully served on many board committees during his tenure as a trustee.

"From my perspective the most important role Clarence has played at Trinity Christian College (and this in no way diminishes his role in fulfilling responsibilities of the other positions he has held) is that he has adopted the business department. For the past fifteen years, he has made sure that the business department, students, and faculty have had the resources to accomplish their goals. The success of the business program and its graduates can be, in a large measure, attributed to the leadership, inspiration, and resources provided by Clarence.

"One of the critical resources that he has provided is the Josephine Davids Memorial Scholarship and the

Clarence Davids and Joyce VanderBent Davids Scholarships. If a program is to be successful, it must have students. And in today's economic environment, many students need financial assistance to pay tuition bills. Clarence had the vision to fill this void by establishing these two endowed scholarship funds that now annually provide eight scholarships to students who meet certain criteria, including:

- Is a business major
- Has a determined financial need
- Exhibits Christian commitment and witness
- Demonstrates positive peer relationships and school involvement
- Has a positive attitude
- Is aggressive and hardworking
- Has a minority background
- Has a average or above-average academic performance

"On the basis of these criteria, the business program has seen students successfully complete the requirements for a business degree and go on to acquire professional positions and prove to be valuable employees. These students uniquely benefited from the inspiration and incentive provided by a financial scholarship during their four years at Trinity Christian College.

"Clarence has also provided a professional classroom environment for the students to learn and work in. He provided the financial resources to remodel and furnish two classrooms in Groot Hall. The rooms are equipped with professional tables and chairs, modern communication resources, and the latest in computerized projection system. The value of these resources is twofold:

1. The faculty has the opportunity to use the most current professional resources to instruct their classes.
2. The students in fulfilling their academic responsibilities can use the same resources as they gain experience and training to become future professionals.

"The business department faculty has also benefited from the concern and generosity of Clarence Davids. He has demonstrated an understanding of the need for faculty to be equipped with current computer technology so that they can be prepared to use it in the classroom and equip future professionals with the skills and abilities they will need to be qualified, professional employees. He has furnished our offices with the current computer hardware and software so that we can go into the classroom appropriately prepared and demonstrate to the students what they will encounter in the "real world of business."

"On May 8, 1998, Trinity Christian College and the business department designed the resources and facilities used by the faculty and students of the business department in Groot Hall as the Clarence Davids, Sr., Business Center. In a small way, this respectfully acknowledges the role he has played in the growth and development of the business program at Trinity Christian College. Clarence has constantly been there to meet the needs of the business department. On an annual basis, he has always come to me with the question, "What do you need?" and he has accepted the challenge and has met those needs.

On June 21, 1999, the business program at Trinity Christian College was accredited by the Association of Business Schools and Programs (ACBSP). Accreditation of our program means that the business program at Trinity Christian College has met and will continue to meet the standards set by the ACBSP for faculty, academic program, and facilities. These are the same standards required of university schools of business and collegiate business programs at academic institutions that are ten to one hundred times larger than the business program at Trinity Christian College. This means that the students who graduate from our business program can compete on a head-to-head basis with the graduates from the larger university and college programs in the employment market. I'm convinced that Clarence's adoption of the business department played a significant role in our ability to become accredited.

"All of the thoughts that I've shared so far relate to the tangible things that Clarence has given to Trinity Christian College, the business program, faculty, and staff. But in the adoption process, the most significant resource that he has shared with us is his faith commitment—his faith in a loving Heavenly Father, who gave His only Son to be our Savior.

"You do not need to spend too much time with Clarence and you will know that he has placed his life in the loving hands of his Heavenly Father, and the focal point of his life is fulfilling his faith commandment. His life is a reflection of Micah 6:8: '. . . and what does the Lord require of you but to do justice, and to love kindness, and to walk humbly with your God.'

"Clarence will readily share with you the fact that he has been blessed—blessed with a loving spouse, children and grandchildren. He has a successful business that God has blessed over the last fifty-plus years and a keen awareness that 'all good and perfect gifts are from above' and that he has the responsibility of using them to the glory of God. So in reality, Clarence sees himself as God's distributor of resources.

"In our conversations through the years, the following exchange of questions and answers took place at some time and place. Clarence was asking and I was answering:

Q: Are there students who have a financial need that might prevent them from going to Trinity Christian College?

A: Yes!

Q: Would an endowment scholarship fund fill their need?

A: Yes!

[Clarence interjects: "Let's set up an endowed scholarship fund, tell me what it takes!"]

Q: What do you need to better prepare the students? Do you need professional classrooms? adequate lighting? ventilation system? computers? software? projection systems?

A: Yes!

Clarence interjects: "What will it take to fill these needs? Give me a wish list and I'll see what I can do."

My response: "This will cost thousands!"

Clarence sums it up: "But, John, the Lord has abundantly blessed me and my family; I'm just giving it back to fill needs in the part of His kingdom located in Palos Heights, Illinois. How soon can you have the wishing list ready?"

"Clarence David's positive, Christian attitude reflects the same warmth and beauty as the evergreen tree that he planted forty years ago. Clarence's enduring spirit and persistent patience has been as refreshing through the years as the cooling shade of the evergreen tree in the courtyard. It has been a personal pleasure to work with him during the past fifteen years as business department chairman, and I prayerfully trust that God will continue to provide him with the health and strength as he continues to work out His plan in Clarence's life."

Turf Builders—Steps to Success:

- Give where the Lord directs and where the need is the greatest, and you will have the success to continue.
- The road to success is garnished with giving—not receiving.
- Never take the glory when it belongs to God.

Chapter Twenty-four

Retirement: A New Work

I always said that I would never retire.

As I search the Bible, I cannot find any mention of this life "condition" or stage. So now that I have reached a point where I turn things over to those younger, what do I call it? Or better yet, what do I do with my life?

I have loved my work in the company, and am very pleased that my son Bill now owns Clarence Davids & Company. It is a well-run business that will continue to prosper and grow with him as the president of the company. However, it is difficult to give up a father-son business no matter how well things are going. It is difficult in giving up the "final say" in the decisions that determine the future of the company and its viability. At the same time, I am extremely proud to see it go on without me.

I can certainly appreciate the inner conflict that people go through to process retirement decisions. I cannot help but think, wonder, and ask myself if Clarence Davids &

Company will go to the third generation of Davids. I would like it if it did, but I have no control over that anymore; only God does.

I know as a Christian that to hold onto the things of this world with a tight fist is to defeat the work of the Lord. I know He always prefers for us to let go—and let God! Our Lord delights in stretching us and moving us into new vistas, and by turning the business over to those I trust, has been, both mentally and physically, a major growing experience for me. I have discovered that in the process of moving away from the affairs of this business, which I created so many years ago, I have had to release my grip and begin to practice the art of holding on with an open hand and a light grasp. At the same time, I have begun to seek the Lord in a new way for the direction of my own life, and I am realizing every day that a new work—not the rocking chair—is in His plans.

Health is a major deciding factor in moving on with my life. Health is always a big "if" as one gets older. Two years ago I underwent triple-bypass heart surgery, which came as one of the biggest surprises of my life. I never thought I had any inclination toward heart disease because no doctor had ever mentioned it before. Now, after the successful surgery, I am told that there is a new blockage that I should be aware of.

Mercifully, the Lord does not show us how many days, weeks, months, or years we have left. I do not know how long I have to live and work as the Lord sees fit, but I am always aware of the question "How should I spend my time?" Should I be making the 3-hour drive into Chicago from Holland, Michigan, to work? There are choices.

As of July 1, 1999, I retired from Clarence Davids & Company. It was an emotional time for me. Bill, my son and owner of the company, has graciously asked me to remain connected to the business with the title of senior sales consultant. I appreciate this very much. I am still always ready to give him advice and support!

One interesting aspect of my new relationship with my son is that we no longer have the business to stand between us in our father-son rapport. Bill started working for me at age thirteen and since then we have always had the business in common to talk about. Now that we do not have the business between us, I may be able to retire from the company, but I need never retire from my work as a father.

I am also glad that I never need to retire from the work of the Lord. It is very important in my life to be active in my spiritual life and church.

So what do I set as a goal for my life? By writing this book, I have accomplished one. Without Joyce I probably would never have done it. She has been my prime motivator in this project. Our marriage continues to be a unique, adventurous, and delightful experience. Joyce and I call it the VanderBent–Davids merger. We are now going on eight years.

I hope to continue some of my volunteer work in our church in the summer Bible club. Helping the mentally impaired has been a blessing for me. I also hope to continue the fine relationship with Trinity Christian College. To help students become educated and use this knowledge in the world is very important to me.

I continue to enjoy my grandchildren and great-grandchildren as well as my stepchildren. Joyce and I have a policy about grandchildren born after our marriage. We have determined in our hearts, and conversation, to drop the "step" and consider these to be "real" grands and great-grands. (For a long time the word "step" hurt us to use, but we have become used to it.) The grandchildren are a delight. I have twelve, and two great-grandchildren.

Another goal is to continue with my "geography lessons" by traveling. Europe and Alaska are calling now, and I am saving Michigan for last (when I get "old") because it is close to home.

There comes a time in one's life that taking "one day at a time" becomes the watchword and a gift from God. In Psalm 90:10*a* it says, "As for the days of our life, they contain seventy years. . . ." I consider any time past seventy as special, and this is doubly true if you are in reasonable health. I thought reaching seventy was a remarkable experience—but now I am seventy-six! A true blessing indeed.

God is so good, and He would have me leave you with this verse from His Scriptures:

> Instruct them to do good, to be rich in good works, to be generous and ready to share, storing up for themselves the treasure of a good foundation for the future, so that they may take hold of that which is life indeed. (1 Tim.6: 18–19)

Godspeed,
Clarence